the **NO-NONSENSE** guide to

CLASS, CASTE & HIERARCHIES

Jeremy Seabrook

KT-437-550

VERSO

About the author

Jeremy Seabrook has written more than 30 books, including, most recently, *Children from Other Worlds*, a comparison of child labor in early 19th-century England and present-day Bangladesh, *Love in a Different Climate* and *Colonies of the Heart*. He has been a teacher, social worker and lecturer, and has written plays for theater, TV and radio. He has contributed to many journals and newspapers, including the **New Internationalist**, Third World Network, *New Statesman* and *The Ecologist*, and at present writes for *The Statesman* in Kolkata (Calcutta).

Acknowledgements

All the people in the poor places of the world from whom I have learned so much about injustice but also hope in the world.

Foreword

The No-Nonsense Guide to Class, Caste and Hierarchies is a fine book, and a welcome addition to Jeremy Seabrook's body of work for which I, like many, am grateful. It is especially valuable in the way it identifies the new class of the rich, the celebrities and others who play 'a significant role in reconciling the poor to their status'.

The fake classlessness of this group was promoted in the 1960s, and this book is, to my knowledge, the first to analyze its illusion in the era of 'globalized' inequalities. The sea change has been the shift in power between capital and labor, and Jeremy Seabrook expertly illuminates this, while leaving us in no doubt that the old system of entrenched power remains in place, ensuring a lack of movement between the classes in spite of the gloss of modern culture and dress. He analyzes the roots of crime, which are frequently exploited by Tony Blair's New Labour as 'a response to an ideology of merit and demerit', and draws a landscape of poverty so often denied by those who promote ideology as economic necessity. This timely, authoritative book is excellent.

John Pilger
Writer and broadcaster
London

the **NO-NONSENSE** guide to

CLASS, CASTE & HIERARCHIES

Jeremy Seabrook

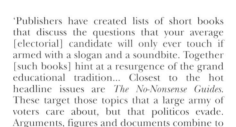

'Publishers have created lists of short books that discuss the questions that your average [electorial] candidate will only ever touch if armed with a slogan and a soundbite. Together [such books] hint at a resurgence of the grand educational tradition... Closest to the hot headline issues are *The No-Nonsense Guides*. These target those topics that a large army of voters care about, but that politicos evade. Arguments, figures and documents combine to prove that good journalism is far too important to be left to (most) journalists.'

Boyd Tonkin,
The Independent,
London

The No-Nonsense Guide to Class, Caste and Hierarchies
First published in the UK by
New Internationalist Publications Ltd
Oxford OX4 1BW, UK
www.newint.org

in association with
Verso
6 Meard Street
London
W1F 0EG
www.versobooks.com

Cover photo: AP Photo / Louisa Buller

Design by New Internationalist Publications Ltd.
Production editor: Troth Wells

Printed by TJ International Ltd, Padstow, Cornwall, UK.

British Library Cataloguing-in-Publication Data.
A catalogue record for this book is available from the British Library.

Library of Congress Cataloguing-in-Publication Data.
A catalogue for this book is available from the Library of Congress.

ISBN 1-85984-465-0

the **NO-NONSENSE** guide to

CLASS, CASTE & HIERARCHIES

CONTENTS

the | **NO-NONSENSE** | guide to

CLASS, CASTE & HIERARCHIES

THE FICTION THAT class has ceased to exist has been spread in a world in which inequality has never been greater. How this can possibly have happened is the subject of this book.

Having been born into a family of leather-workers in an English town, it was impossible for me to ignore the issue of class: our town was saturated with stories of poverty and oppression, and of the efforts by the people to create some kind of resistance through the trade unions and working-class institutions. As the first member of my family ever to have gone to university, it was easy to judge the gulf between my place of origin and my presumed destination. A deep revulsion against the injustice of lives of struggle and lives of privilege has animated all my work since then.

I never believed all the rhetoric about the dismantling of class society. This scepticism was part of the inheritance from the old shoe-making people of my youth: they were instinctive egalitarians, unimpressed by social status, dissidents against the prevailing orthodoxies of their age.

Of course class differences became blurred, between a decaying industrial working class and a growing middle class within my own country. It was simply that in an era of globalization, class was being reconfigured on a world-wide scale. The relative improvements within Britain were won only at the expense of millions of people drawn into an 'integrated' global economy, just as we had been drawn into the manufacturing industry of early industrial society. Recognizing this as a familiar process has helped to keep alive a sense that what is happening to the factory workers of Bangladesh or Indonesia and the maidservants in Manila or Mumbai [Bombay] does not make them victims of some remote and incomprehensible process. They are our own recognizable kin, separated from us only by a moment in time, a different culture, another climate.

We are deceived if we think the creation of wealth can dissolve inequalities. We are under an illusion if we imagine that relationships between rich and poor can be altered without profound structural change. Beneath the gaudy and noisy surfaces of globalism, we are caught up in enduring patterns of dominance and subordination. It is time to call things once more by their proper names.

The rich Western societies declare themselves dedicated to equality of opportunity for women, ethnic minorities, those of diverse sexual orientation and people with disability. These aspirations to equality are both a substitute for and an avoidance of addressing more profound inequalities; the widening gap between rich and poor, both within countries and between countries. Unless we can retrieve some sense of the structural relationship between rich and poor, the incompatibility of their interests in a world of finite resources, there is little hope of change in the world.

The ghost of Marx haunts the discussions of social justice and equality of the anti-globalization movement. The failure of Communism does not invalidate Marx's analysis of the position of the exploiters and the oppressed. A world remains to be won; but it is an older, less idealistic, more sober and more damaged world than anything envisaged by the early opponents of the injuries of class.

Jeremy Seabrook
London

1 What are 'class' and 'inequality'?

The historical context of class... showing how it was defined by industrialism... and how it has been replaced and re-defined as 'inequality'

ALL SOCIETIES ARE stratified in one way or another, in hierarchies of power and wealth. The few egalitarian exceptions, of indigenous and tribal peoples, have been destroyed or degraded by contact with the modern world. Privilege has many methods of self-preservation, not least physical force, but sometimes through a mystical appeal to the special intellectual or spiritual powers the privileged claim to possess. Some societies are built on slavery, most upon the oppression of those who perform the most vital labor of that society. Throughout history, there have been struggles of the oppressed against their 'superiors', although even when the 'natural' order has been overthrown, it has rarely been long before new powerful groups established their own supremacy, their own lineage, their own religion or power over others.

At the time of the Industrial Revolution social classes became more sharply antagonistic, as older mystiques legitimating social stratification decayed, and the rich confronted the poor in stark antagonism. Social class, in its contemporary understanding, was defined primarily in Europe. The United States, with its egalitarian origins in reaction against the feudal order of Europe, saw itself as liberated from archaic categories of aristocracy and the lower orders. It was only later that the profound inequalities of slavery were addressed, and while the idea of class remained foreign to the US tradition, institutionalized social injustice has persisted. Today this is discussed in terms of 'inequality' rather than of opposing social classes. The modern idea of class was born in Europe, became an obsession in Britain and was denied in the United States.

This book reflects on the origins of class in contemporary society; its apparent disappearance and periodical re-discovery in one way or another, most recently in the emergence of a global class system, as a result of globalization.

Global inequality

According to the United Nations *Human Development Report*[1], the world's richest 20 per cent receive 86 per cent of the world's gross product; the middle 60 per cent 13 per cent, while the poorest 20 per cent receive one per cent. The ratio between the incomes of the top and bottom fifth of humanity is 74 to 1. In 1960 it was 30 to 1.

But there is another story, which perhaps helps to explain why these often quoted, extreme inequalities are not only tolerated by the peoples of the world, but regarded as part of the natural order of things; why, in other words, there is so little pressure to resist the continuously growing economic injustice in the world.

Datamonitor UK also notes that there are nearly 4 million people (that is, 8 per cent of the population over 16 years of age) who have liquid assets of between $45,000 (£30,000) and $300,000 (£200,000).[2] The numbers in this group have been growing by 12 per cent a year for the past five years. Their wealth consists of cash or shares, before the value of any property or pension funds they hold is taken into account.

A survey based on fieldwork from the Office for National Statistics found that at the end of 1999, 26 per cent of the British population was living in poverty, measured in terms of low income and multiple deprivation of necessities. This pattern is repeated (with minor variations) in all industrialized countries.

Wealth and poverty

- 1.3 billion people lack access to clean water; 1.2 billion live on less than a dollar a day; 840 million are malnourished.
- More than 20,000 people die each day from hunger-related diseases.
- The assets of the world's 200 richest individuals more than doubled between 1994 and 1998 to over $1 trillion.
- The richest three people in the world have assets greater than the combined output of the 48 poorest countries.
- In the 1990s, 55 countries experienced real per capita income decrease.
- There are around 7 million millionaires in the world, half of them in the US.
- 12 of the 20 richest people in the world are Americans.
- Independent market analysis research from Datamonitor in Britain[2], states that the number of millionaires in Britain is growing at the rate of 17 per cent a year; and by 2001 there were 74,000 millionaires.
- Data from the UK's Office for National Statistics stated that 1999-2000 saw the highest gap between rich and poor yet recorded. The poorest fifth of households had 6 per cent of national income after tax, while the share held by the top fifth rose from 44 to 45 per cent.

Global rich

There exists a global rich class, made up of inheritors of wealth, but increasingly of celebrities, entrepreneurs, the makers of spectacular fortunes, the new rich of Information Technology, life-sciences and the recipients of other recent technological windfalls, sports and media stars, musicians and show-people. There is also a fast-growing and powerful global middle class. This serves, in one way or another, the process of the creation of surplus value, or profit, often for big transnational corporations and the bureaucracies that support them. These people are a significant force in the world. Their role is twofold. They offer a model to the aspiring poor, and they help police poverty: for privilege, even modest privilege, may expand and grow only if the gap between rich and poor is maintained, or increased, as is the case in almost every country in the world.

Inequality is an abstraction. Its great advantage to the rich is that it replaces earlier concepts of class. These were embodied in real living figures of flesh and blood and their relationship to each other. Inequality is a statistical term, in which the participants appear only as victims or beneficiaries. If human beings have any part to play in remedies for inequality, these will be highly qualified experts and professionals. Ordinary people are absent from inequality; in class relationships the people are omnipresent.

Growing inequality

The UN *Human Development Report* tells only part of the story. For the 60 per cent in the middle who receive the 13 per cent of income are by no means a homogeneous group. Their inclusion as a single entity is misleading, for it implies that only the bottom 20 per cent are poor – those living on less than a dollar a day. But *three billion* people live on less than $2 a day and far more than that on less than $5 a day. So the figures that lump together 60 per cent need to be broken down to give a clearer picture, not only of the extremes – which are shocking enough – but also of the inequalities hidden by the bulging 'middle'.

These figures are widely published, accessible, and in whatever form they are presented, they lead to the same conclusion. Growing inequality is continuously monitored by international institutions, and by academic establishments within countries. There is no attempt to conceal or justify this process. It is just the way things are.

This acceptance of inequality is at odds with a world which constantly advertises its miracles of technology, its mastery of the secrets of nature, its capacity for transforming the lives of the people. The global economy creates the impression of a busy, restless, can-do culture sweeping with irresistible force across the face of the earth. Nothing, it seems, can withstand the impact of the communications revolution, the conquest of space, breakthroughs in medicine, the mapping of the human genome, and all the other promises of emancipation for humanity. Why are governments and international institutions apparently impotent when confronted by the widening divide between rich and poor? In a world where everything is possible, why should this central issue present such a difficult problem?

This book addresses the well-recorded facts of social injustice, but also asks why it is not contested more strongly. Why do the poor accept an arbitrary withholding from them of the necessities of life, when the rich take for themselves a disproportionate share of the wealth of the world? This question requires an understanding of the history – and continuing existence – of class relationships, and their reconfiguration in the wake of globalization. For social classes have not been eliminated by the treacherous continuum of inequality, but have been remade, often in ways which make them obscure to the participants. The story (and it is a story) is a simple one; yet it consists of layers of complexity and *complicatedness*, which sometimes make it difficult to follow the thread.

Why 'class' became crucial

Class stratification means the division of society into unequal strata or groups. The differences between them express social relationships and constitute the social identity of the members of each group. Some mobility between classes is usually possible. Caste, on the other hand, ascribes a position to people usually through birth, and it is more difficult for individuals to move beyond the inherited position in the caste hierarchy. There are elements of both class and caste in most societies. (We return to the differences between class and caste in Chapter 8).

Discussions of class in industrial society have been colored by philosopher Karl Marx, who reduced class interests to two – the owners of capital and those who

The 20 richest people in the world, 2000

Lists are produced each year of the wealthiest people; each list has a slightly different order but the same names crop up with astonishing regularity.

		Value (US $ billions)	Country	Age	Source of wealth
1	Gates, Bill	58.7	US	45	Microsoft
2	Buffett, Warren	32.3	US	70	investments
3	Allen, Paul	30.4	US	48	Microsoft
4	Ellison, Larry	26.0	US	56	Oracle computers
5	Albrecht, Theo & Karl	25.0	Germany	—	supermarkets
6	Prince Alaweed Bin Talal	20.0	Saudi Arabia	44	investments
7	Walton, Jim	18.8	US	53	Wal-Mart
8	Walton, John	18.7	US	55	Wal-Mart
9	Walton, Robson	18.6	US	57	Wal-Mart
10	Walton, Alice	18.5	US	52	Wal-Mart
11	Walton, Helen	18.5	US	81	Wal-Mart
12	Quandt, Joanna	17.8	Germany	74	BMW
13	Ballmer, Steve	16.6	US	45	Microsoft
14	Thomson, Kenneth	16.4	Canada	77	publishing
15	Bettencourt, Liliane	15.6	France	75	L'Oréal
16	Anschutz, Philip	15.3	Sweden	75	Ikea
18	Redstone, Sumner	12.6	US	78	Viacom
18	Li Ka Ly	12.6	Hong Kong	73	diversified
20	Kirch, Leo	12.0	Germany	74	media

Forbes 500.

have nothing but their labor-power to sell. It is the objective of the former to make profit out of the surplus value produced by the workers. The relationship is exploitative, antagonistic and, according to Marx, highly unstable. It must lead to conflict, which will end either in the triumph of the workers or in the ruin of the contending classes – the famous choice between socialism and barbarism.

The word 'class', meaning the economic and social position of groups of people, is of fairly recent origin. Its present-day use dates from the mid-18th century. Its roots are in the Latin, *classis*, referring to the six orders the Romans were divided into for the purposes of taxation. Before the idea of class became significant in the West, concepts of *rank* and *station* described the social position of individuals. In Britain, the word *order* – dating from around 1300 – indicated the collective position of groups of people.

In the medieval world, society was divided into *estates*. They comprised three legal classifications – the nobility, the clergy and the common people. 'Class' came into usage in France, partly as a consequence of the work of the *Encyclopédistes*, a group of 18th-century French intellectuals, who attempted to assemble all the knowledge available to the modern world. This led them to systematic classification of plants, animals and minerals and phenomena of the natural world. It was then a short step to apply the methodology to the social and economic position of individuals in society. In Britain, the philanthropist Jonas Hanway was the first to refer to the 'lower classes of people' in 1772. The economist Adam Smith, in his *Wealth of Nations* (1776), used the word class in a general sense, but when he spoke of the division of labor, with its different functions, he spoke of 'the ranks and conditions' of people in society.

The concept of *class* fitted in with changes brought about by industrial society, and it gained wide currency with early industrialism in the first half of the 19th century. The medieval idea of estates had suggested an organic relationship. Classes, although mutually dependent, were also antagonistic; it was Marx who elevated this clash into his fateful theory of irreconcilable interests between *bourgeoisie* and *proletariat*. Marx specifically stated that class was an expression of a relationship to the means of production – the capitalists who owned the mills, mines and factories, and the workers who had nothing but their labor-power to sell.

The origins of the word proletariat are in the Latin *proletarii*. This referred to the poorest classes, those whose only resources lay in their offspring. The word found its way into French in the 18th century, but occurred in its modern sense in English only in 1853, when it was used disparagingly of the lowest classes.

Bourgeois has a more complicated history. From Latin *burgus* and German *Burg*, meaning a town under the protection of a castle, it came to mean citizen in medieval France, as opposed to peasant or noble. The word was used in France to indicate the mercantile middle class (those involved in trade and commerce) from the 17th century. Before the revolution, the nobility used the word as a term of contempt towards those whose money they certainly did not despise. Both words – *bourgeois* and *proletarian* – still have an alien sound to English speakers.

What's in a name?

In Britain, definitions of class continued to be influenced by older ideas of rank, despite the social upheaval of industrialization. The lower orders, the laboring classes and the middling ranks of society existed alongside the aristocracy and gentry. As the stratification of industrial society became more rigid, these definitions settled into the now familiar classification of upper, middle and working *class*.

The discrepancy in these categories was pointed out by philosopher and social critic Raymond Williams[3]. He wrote: 'Most people in Britain think of themselves as "middle class" or "working class". But the first point to make is that these are not true alternatives. The alternatives to "middle" are "lower" and "upper"; the alternative to "working" is "independent" or "propertied". The wonderful muddle we are now in springs mainly from this confusion, that one term has a primarily social, the other a primarily economic reference.'

'Middle' suggests simply a position in society. 'Working' suggests a function. This helps, perhaps, to explain why a 'working class' has become virtually invisible in the contemporary Western world. In the US in particular, but increasingly in Europe also, this is a category in which people decreasingly recognize themselves. US politicians regularly refer to the 'middle classes' and sometimes to 'working people', but mention of a 'working class' is said to turn people off.

The idea of a growing middle class expresses a relationship not so much to the means of production, as to *other people*. It introduces an element of *status*, which derives from sociologist Max Weber's efforts to define more clearly the complexity of expanding industrial society towards the end of the 19th century, a time when the wider range of economic possibilities blurred the easy classification of capitalists and workers. For Weber, class is multi-dimensional, and includes both the relationship to the means of production and to the means of consumption. Class becomes more diffuse and complex.

In the United States, the idea of 'working class', although it figured in politics, was virtually absent from academic discussion until the Great Depression in the mid-20th century. It is a paradox that the most advanced capitalist society dispensed with categories which Marx and most European commentators regarded as vital to discussion of social relationships in industrial societies. Status replaced class as the key

---

The US and the Mystery of the Disappearing Working Class

The working class has been believed, ever since Marx, to be inseparable from working-class organization. From the relative weakness of such movements in the US (although of course there were many activists and struggles) it has been concluded that the working class scarcely exists. In a country marked by continuous diversity of migration, other struggles and identities have taken priority – people have seen themselves as black, Jewish, Irish, Italian, Hispanic before they see themselves as working class. In 2001, more than 30.5 million Americans were born outside the country – more than 11 per cent of the population. The ideology of the Americanization of immigrants has been a more powerful unifying force than perceptions of class; especially to those who saw the US as a destination, a haven from poverty and persecution elsewhere.

indicator on the continuum of rich and poor in the US. Status was acquired through power rather than power through status: the American belief that anyone can rise from humble origins to become President of the US continued to exercise a powerful hold over the imagination even when it had clearly become myth (most US Presidents have come from wealthy, often highly privileged backgrounds).

Even so, the US promised freedoms that would wipe out European hierarchies. It offered greater opportunities to get rich and to consume than were available to the majority in Europe. In the US, moreover, the proportion of people in the industrial sector never reached levels seen in early industrial Britain. The growth of 'middle class' occupations stifled the emergence of a dominant 'working class' consciousness.

Rich as Rockefeller

In the period since the Second World War, the positional aspect of status has supplanted the functional aspect of class for many (former working-class) people in Europe as well as in the US. Sociologist Vance Packard suggested people were ceasing to identify themselves as members of this or that social class, but were creating a new sense of belonging through objects of consumption[4]. Communities of shared tastes and lifestyles were being defined against those of different (lower or higher) patterns of expenditure. 'Status', in contemporary society, is close to 'station' in pre-industrial hierarchies, with the important difference that 'station' implies socially fixed positions, while 'status'-oriented society is extremely mobile. The jackpot winner, the singer with the hit record, the TV star and the successful entrepreneur can surround themselves with the trappings of luxury as fast as they can buy them.

In pre-industrial society, it was acknowledged that 'birth' or 'breeding' distinguished those at the top of the social pyramid. The upper classes were separated from the 'lower orders' by the 'middling rank' of society. In status-conscious societies, objects of conspicuous consumption are identified with forms of honor, which formerly clustered around other characteristics – inherited position, property, military prowess. The contemporary iconography of high status is more open – anyone who can afford it can go through the obligatory shopping list of ornate villas with tight security, champagne and caviar, diamonds, yachts, Rolls Royce cars, Armani suits and accessories bearing the 'correct' brand-name.

Before industrialization, social belonging was a function simply of position in society. It was only with the Industrial Revolution that a working class – or proletariat, as Marx called it – emerged. The fact that the *function* of this class is its principal characteristic suggests that industrial labor was a profoundly disruptive force. It was destined not only to disturb social hierarchies which had persisted since the feudal times of the Middle Ages (c800-1300) but also to overshadow the antagonism which had grown between the old aristocracy of landed classes and the class of entrepreneurs who were, by the end of the 18th century, knocking at the doors of political power and privilege.

Forever feudal

Feudalism was essentially a caste system, and is significant because it still characterizes many agrarian societies in the world. It lays the groundwork for the structures of class, caste and hierarchies that exist today. To find out about it, we step back in time to the Middle Ages in England.

The word 'feudal' comes from the same root as the German word 'Vieh', meaning cattle; reflecting an earlier nomadic society in which cattle were the principal source of wealth. The king stood at the apex, above a strongly hierarchical system of landed dependency. Lords obtained land for past services (mainly military) and in expectation of similar future loyalty. The *vassal* was the personal follower of his immediate lord. Lords granted land to their vassals not in ownership, but in *usufruct* which means they had access to the produce of that land. This was granted originally on a personal basis, but eventually became hereditary. The land held by a vassal was the expression of an invisible bond to his superior. Lords had power to hold their own courts, a power derived ultimately from the king. This secular hierarchy was paralleled by a religious one of bishops and priests and monks – the second 'estate' of the three great estates that constituted medieval society.

Feudalism was eroded in the late Middle Ages by the growth of towns and the rise of a money-based, rather than a land-based economy. It became impracticable for lords to retain knights in their service waiting for the call of war. The knights commuted their military obligations for money; and eventually money replaced land as a symbol of power. Similarly, the emancipation of *villeins* (*serfs* or tied peasants cultivating a lord's land) grew, and tenure by service gave way to tenure by rent – the lord's fields were tilled by hired laborers.

The Black Death wiped out surplus labor; it became impossible legally to bind labor to the soil. Villeins escaped from their own lords to become laborers for hire. Lords became landlords, and villeins landless laborers. Although birth remained the principal determinant of status, the growth of mercantilism – merchants and trading – and manufacturing led to a steady accession of the particularly talented into higher ranks of society, usually by means of royal and political patronage. But until the industrial era, the sense of hierarchy persisted: the superior, middle and lower ranks in society.

Privilege prevails

Privilege in every society spins myths to legitimize its power or its monopoly over resources. Ruling castes or classes perpetuate themselves by a mystical appeal to antiquity, lineage, divine sanction or 'breeding', which justify their right to rule. Historian Walter Bagehot[5] claimed that the nobility preserves a country from too great a worship of money, and that reverence for rank is less base than reverence for money. In 1835, after the passage of the 1832 Reform Bill, British Prime Minister Benjamin Disraeli wrote: 'For nearly five centuries the hereditary Peerage... has formed an active and powerful branch of our legislature... No statesman can doubt that the peculiar character of the hereditary branch of our legislature has mainly contributed to the stability of our institutions, and to the order and prosperous security which that stability has produced. Nor can we forget that the hereditary principle has at all times secured a senate for this country inferior in intelligence to no political assembly on record...'[6] He refers to 'an ancient people, who have made inheritance the pervading principle of their social polity, who are proud of their old families and fond of their old laws'.

An idealized version of hierarchical relationships reinforced the British idea of its own past; this took root, paradoxically, in the psyche of the industrial bourgeoisie, who made their fortunes out of manufacture. Historian Martin Wiener[7] speaks of the 'consolidation of a "gentrified" bourgeois culture, particularly the rooting of pseudo-aristocratic attitudes and values in upper-middle class educated opinion'. Wiener sees this as harmful to economic efficiency and a cause of the relative economic decline of Britain. However that may be, it is remarkable that whatever the disdain for financial gain on the part of the old nobility, they managed to salvage a great deal of their material advantage, as well as their power and honor, in the generations after the Industrial Revolution.

In the end, the interests of the nobility merged with those of the new moneyed middle class; a compromise born of expediency, especially when confronted by a rising working class. The heritage of the old rich was maintained by the wealth of the new, a marriage of convenience.

In our time, this has yielded to a more overt stratification by money, exemplified by pop stars and sports heroes – people like Madonna or Magic Johnson – where money and talent create a new class of celebrities, which is honored and admired – and plays a significant role in reconciling the poor to their status. These people have, in some measure, replaced the aristocracy and monarchy. The decline in reverence for the royal family in Britain reflects this change: positions derived from birth no longer inspire the respect commanded by wealth from the intensive marketing of talent, youth and glamour. The Spice Girls pop group, five women who answered a newspaper advertisement in the early 1990s, had personal fortunes by 2001 of at least $33 million (£22 million) each. This rise of exceptional individuals is of course familiar in the US where people were founding their own plutocratic – wealth makes them powerful – dynasties, while British entrepreneurs aped the aristocracy.

Not that the old ruling class has become impoverished. Among the richest people in the world, the Queen of England, the Sultan of Brunei and the King of Saudi Arabia are still present, along with Bill Gates and other representatives of spectacular contemporary enterprise. The wealth of the Duke of Westminster amounts to $5.6 billion (£3.75 billion). If the private assets of the Queen are included, she is probably among the 20 richest people in the world.

The Rich List, compiled each year by the London *Sunday Times*, recorded an increase between 1999 and 2000 of almost $47 billion (£31 billion) in the wealth of the thousand richest people in Britain. Of these, 'only' 258 inherited their millions, compared with two-thirds in 1989. Whether wealth is old or new is rather academic in a world in which inequality is growing so spectacularly.

1 *United Nations Development Report*, UNDP/OUP 2000. **2** Datamonitor, United Kingdom, 2001. **3** *The Long Revolution*, Raymond Williams, Chatto and Windus 1961. **4** *The Status Seekers*, Vance Packard, 1959, Bedford/St Martin's Press 1995. **5** *The English Constitution*, Walter Bagehot, 1904 (cited in *The English Ruling Class*, WL Guttsman, Weidenfeld and Nicholson 1969). **6** 'A Vindication of the English Constitution' in *Whigs and Whiggism: Political Writings*, Benjamin Disraeli, London 1913. **7** *English Culture and the Decline of the Industrial Spirit 1850-1980*, Martin Wiener, Penguin 1985.

2 The importance of a working class

Why the emergence of a working class has influenced all discussion on class in industrial society... Why class remained relatively subordinate in societies like the US, while in others – notably in Russia – it became the central reality of society... Class consciousness: what makes people aware or oblivious of their class position?

THIS SECTION DRAWS mainly on the example of Britain, as the first country to industrialize. It was the first to re-shape its class system into the pattern that later became familiar to all industrial societies: an upper layer of traditional élites, landowners or aristocrats, a growing middle class of entrepreneurs, a working class (a phenomenon never before seen in the world), and below them, the poor, many of them casualties of industrialization.

The startling new element was the working class: concentrations of people in industrial towns and cities, usually serving only one mechanized industry – mining, cotton, wool, leather, metal, brass and so on. The places where these people lived caused great anxiety to the ruling classes, the more so since the growth of manufacturing industry quickened so soon after the French Revolution (1789). This had produced 'among the higher orders... a horror of every kind of innovation'. That excesses similar to those in France – the hounding of the aristocracy and the execution of the Queen – might be contemplated by the laboring poor in Britain underlay much of the penal legislation of the last decade of the 18th century and the early years of the 19th. At least 63 capital offenses were added between 1760 and 1810 to the almost two hundred already in existence. Historian EP

The importance of a working class

Thompson noted that 'not only petty theft, but primitive forms of industrial rebellion – destroying a silk loom, throwing down fences when commons were enclosed, and firing corn ricks – were to be punished by death'[1].

The fear of what might be simmering in the minds of the ragged half-starved miners in their squalid habitations, wandering gangs of laborers or cotton operatives, was strengthened by riots over the price of bread or against new machinery. As time went by, and the new industrial society began to define itself, the 18th-century 'king and country' mob merged into anti-industrial movements like Luddism. A defining moment came with the Peterloo Massacre in 1819, when thousands of weavers demonstrating in Manchester were cut down by the military: 11 died and many hundreds were injured; more than 100 women and girls either cut by sabers, or trampled by horses' hooves.

Why the 'working class' became central

The Combination Acts (1799-1800) outlawed trade unionism, and although these were repealed in 1824, the specter of organization by the workers remained. This led to a far greater degree of combining by the propertied classes than anything achieved by their laborers. The protection of privilege was highly institutionalized throughout the 19th century – land ownership, entrance to Oxford and Cambridge universities, the Civil Service, the army officer corps and the established Church. The subsequent opening up of privilege permitted a wider range of class origins in recruits to these institutions, but the values these represent remain unchanged.

There was great confusion and anxiety in the early years of industrial society. Government placed spies and informers among all groups believed to harbor radical sentiments. People streamed into towns and cities, squatting in makeshift slums, tramping to the quasi-military rhythm of the factory system. The landscape was transformed by the new towns; factory chimneys scribbled their enigmatic messages of an unimaginable future against Britain's cloudy skies. In 1750, there had been only two cities with a population of more than 50,000. In 1801 there were eight; by 1851, twenty-nine.

In the 1840s the German philosopher Friedrich Engels published his powerful evocation of the manufacturing districts[2]. Much of the material had already been overtaken by a number of reforms – for example Public Health legislation had addressed some of the worst excesses of industrial squalor. But the book's interest now lies principally in its depiction

---

Working-class life

In the late 19th century there emerged a distinctive pattern of working-class life in Britain. According to Marx's definition – that an individual's relationship to the means of production determines his/her class – the working class would have comprised more than three-quarters of the population of England by the late 19th century. A particular culture grew: defensive and in-turned, characterized by life in densely-built streets, with chapels, factories and pubs on the corner; by the tramp of boots on the pavement in the morning, small plots of garden land (allotments), 'friendly societies' for savings and loans, brass bands, Sundays in the park, the music-hall and later the local cinema.

It was a highly ritualized, often oppressive life, particularly for women; but when there was a disaster in the pit or a factory fire, the women and children who gathered in the darkness were united in fear, and not only because they might lose the only source of livelihood they had. This way of life persisted from the 1870s until 1945; punctuated by depression, unemployment, periods of prosperity and times of war. It strengthened the sense of a common fate, and led to a sub-political solidarity in the face of insecurity and loss. The women who washed the dead and brought children into the world, the daily witness of injustice and the cruelty of officials, overseers and employers, the wisdom born of poverty and want, the ingenuity deployed in the art of survival – this created a storehouse of resources which people drew upon for both practical support and moral succor. Industrial life was a harsh and cruel visitation, but the response of the people was more often than not dignified and humane. ■

of the infernal landscapes of early urban and industrial conditions – conditions seen today in the cities of the Third World. Engels' description of Manchester's river Irk and surrounds prefigures present-day grim scenes from Dharavi in Mumbai, Nova Iguaçu near Rio de Janeiro or Bekasi in Jakarta: 'At the bottom flows, or rather stagnates, the Irk, a narrow coal-black, foul-smelling stream, full of debris and refuse which it deposits on the shallower right bank. In dry weather, a long string of the most disgusting blackish-green slime pools are left standing on the bank, from the depths of which bubbles of miasmic gas constantly arise and give forth a stench unendurable even on the bridge forty or fifty feet above the surface of the stream... Above the bridge are tanneries, bone-mills and gas-works, from which all drains and refuse find their way into the Irk, which receives further the contents of all the neighboring sewers and privies. Below the bridge... each house is packed close behind its neighbor...'

Just what kind of humanity might be produced by such landscapes haunted the imagination of their rulers throughout the century. These rulers would have felt more secure had they realized that insurrectionary fantasies were, for the most part, far from the sensibility of the people. Working-class discontent was exploited by middle-class agitators in favor of the Reform Bill of 1832, which gave the vote to the new entrepreneurial class. Soon afterwards, it became clear to the workers' leaders that they had been merely numbers in the struggle. The Reform Bill distanced working-class radicals from those with whom they had been allied; and gave a clear impulse to a distinctive consciousness. 'In radical terms,' noted EP Thompson, 'in 1832 the "people" became the "working classes". It was widely believed that the replacement of an aristocracy of title by an aristocracy of wealth – or the fusion of the two, "in an unholy coalition against the happiness of the great majority" –

had led to an even more oppressive system, which denied the worker "a fair subsistence".'

The Chartists

The most significant working-class organization in the first half of the 19th century was Chartism (from the Charter, a list of constitutional reforms drawn up by the movement). There was a 'moral force' faction (of the non-industrial radical artisans of London and Birmingham) and 'physical force' faction (of northern factory workers and hard-pressed handloom weavers who had nothing to lose). Contemporaries saw it as the political expression of the new industrial class, fueled by hunger, distress and the strange social and economic convulsions that had called it into existence.

Labor historian Gareth Stedman Jones[3] points out the anomaly that unemployment and poverty led to a movement for radical constitutional demands and universal suffrage rather than for relief from the State. He quotes RG Gammage, historian of Chartism, who wrote that 'the masses look on the enfranchised classes, whom they behold reposing on their couch of opulence, and contrast that opulence with the misery of their own condition. Reasoning from effect to cause there is no marvel that they arrive at the conclusion – that their exclusion from political power is the cause of our social anomalies.' This tradition of working indirectly for economic improvement through political reform has continued to the present; and only in the past two decades has the power of local (ie national) governments – in relation to globalization – been called into question.

The ideas of social reformer Robert Owen influenced working-class movements in Britain chiefly through his abhorrence of competition, which he regarded as an immoral and unnatural process[4]. He believed all classes should unite in rejection of its unwholesome tyranny. Political change would do nothing without this moral transformation. Owen made no distinction between the rich, in pursuit of futile luxury, and the poor, in pursuit of simple survival. He shunned ideas of class conflict in favor of unity in the pursuit of universal happiness and a new moral world. In this sense, he shared the values that were to characterize American industrial society, as well as prefiguring much of the later labor movement in Britain.

A majority of the working class never moved beyond a constitutionalist respect for certain conventions and traditions. Such a cautious, even conservative, structure of feeling in the British working class told decisively in the defeat of revolutionary ideas; and it permanently marginalized the Communist Party. EP Thompson examines in detail the effects of Methodism on the radicalism of the working class. The consolations of religion, with the promise of justice in the kingdom of heaven, may have assisted in the maintenance of social peace; but the organization of trade unions and Left political parties owes much to the dissenting chapels and the effective administration they established.

Chartism, after the presentation of its monster petition at the great meeting on Kennington Common in 1848, quickly faded. The spectacular growth and expansion of mid-Victorian Britain, the beginning of which coincided with the Great Exhibition of 1851, led to steady material improvements for most of the people for almost a quarter of a century. The decay of radical movements and increasing pace of reform led to social peace that almost exactly prefigures the era of prosperity a hundred years later – from the early 1950s to the oil crisis of 1973. In the mid years of the 19th century, the wealth of Britain increasingly attached working people to the existing order, just as consumerism did a century later.

Early labor unions

Labor historian Gareth Stedman Jones states that if 'the making of the English working class' took place in the

1790-1830 period, something akin to a remaking of the working class occurred in the years between 1870 and 1900. This was marked by growth of the 'new unionism', that is general labor unions; the organization of the casual and unskilled, most of whom had previously been beyond the scope of 'craft unionism.' They included dockers/longshoremen and gas-workers, who later formed the Transport and General Workers' Union and the General and Municipal Workers, which made up one-quarter of organized labor in Britain by the late 1940s. The social and organizational experience gathered in the early industrial period were taken forward into trade union activity. This gave rise to the Labour Representation Committee, which subsequently became the Labour Party.

This was paralleled by one of the most potent moments of working-class organization in the US – the founding of the Industrial Workers of the World (IWW) in 1905. This was in opposition to the American Federation of Labor (AFL) headed by Samuel Gompers, whose emphasis was on organizing skilled rather than unskilled labor. The IWW was to be the 'One Big Union', a movement of all workers in all industries, which would work towards universal liberation from wage slavery. They became known as

The case of Eugene Debs

Eugene Debs was one of the heroes of American socialism. Born in Terre Haute, Indiana, in 1855, the oldest son of immigrants from Alsace, he left school at 14 to work in the railroad shops. He founded the American Railway Union, which was destroyed in the violent Pullman Strike of 1894. He served six months in jail in 1895 and was 'converted to socialism'. He ran for President five times as a socialist, and in 1912, received 6 per cent of the vote. Opposing the entry of the US to the First World War, which was seen as treasonous, his citizenship was revoked and he was sentenced to 10 years in prison. From the Atlanta penitentiary he ran for President again in 1920, and won 3.5 per cent of the vote. His sentence was commuted by President Harding in 1921, but his citizenship was never restored. He died in 1926. ■

the 'Wobblies'. Although it split into two bitter factions it reached the height of its power between 1912 and 1917. Its principal strength lay in lumber workers of the Pacific North-West, migratory workers from the wheatfields of the central states, textile workers in the North East, longshoremen and mineworkers. Among often violent strikes were those of the miners in Goldfield, Nevada (1906-7), textile workers in Lawrence, Massachusetts (1912) and silk workers in Paterson, NJ (1913). They opposed the entry of the US into the First World War, as a result of which many leaders and rank and file members were imprisoned. The 'Red Scare' of communism in 1920 undermined the effectiveness of the Wobblies, when 'criminal syndicalism' was outlawed in many states.

Working-class culture

The difference between the life of the late 19th century and the turbulence of the Chartist period was that the working class had become installed in industrial life, and had made their peace with it. During the early 19th century, industrialism was unfamiliar. The quarrel of radicals was with the State itself – the monarchy, the legislature, the Church, bureaucracy and the magistracy. They believed these things could be replaced by popular, more democratic structures. Industrial society itself was widely perceived as an aberration, reversible. By the mid-century it appeared permanent. This was the system in which people had to make their home. The transformation of capitalism into cosmos had begun.

The two or three generations born to this way of life seemed to show that the working class had come to terms with and made its home in industrial society. This led to what is called the 'culturalist' view; the attribution of certain values to the working class: a strong sense of community and collective values, a world of mutuality and sharing. It was suggested that these represented the 'essence' of the working class.

It is misleading to speak of 'the working class' as a homogeneous group. It was always characterized by hierarchies of labor, highly-skilled artisans separated by a wide gulf of living standards and attitudes towards education, from unskilled and general laborers. There was a sharp distinction between the 'respectable' and the 'rough' working class, sometimes living close together, confined to the poorest areas. Some of the most degrading work fell on women and children, especially in the early industrial period. The conditions of domestic service maintained millions of young women in abject servitude. Most married women were not expected to work. Their life was oppressive, many tethered by marriage to men who abused and beat them and failed to give them enough money to provide for the family. But the common experience tended towards unity rather than separation, not necessarily in the political sense, but rather in recognizing that insecurity, unemployment and sickness were certainties in life, and that there was no other remedy than mutual help and support.

In the United States, it was a similar picture: newcomers, of whatever ethnic group, lived in the same tenements, performed the same work in sweatshops, suffered the same material deprivation. The only difference in the US was that as one group became more prosperous, new waves of migrants took their place, and inherited, as it were, a similar way of life. Thus the survivors of slavery, Irish, Jews, Italians, Puerto Ricans, Mexicans have all followed the same path. This process is visible today all over the world. A new urban working class has come into being; and people are always poor in the same way. The insecurity and threat from industrial life to health, well-being and even survival, act as more powerful forces in most communities than characteristics which divide people.

The final blow to the idea of a specifically 'working-class culture' came in Britain with the coalminers' strike of 1984-5. The miners had always roused strong feelings and were seen as emblematic of the working class – heroic figures, in the forefront of struggle against exploitation, the root of the labor movement. The strike was against pit closures and the loss of tens of thousands of jobs. The battles between police and miners were of shocking brutality: the miners were represented as violent wreckers, as an undemocratic force set against a legitimate government. Support groups all over the country gave material help to the strikers. Women played a crucial part in the resistance: many miners' wives toured the country, eloquent and passionate, seeking support and resources to continue the fight. Most strikers were aghast that what they saw as a legitimate defense of their jobs could be portrayed as a threat to constitutional order. After their defeat, the rump of the industry was privatized. The miners dwindled in number to only a few thousand, a shadow of the million in 1914. After that, there was little doubt that the 'classic' working class had reached a final stage in its dissolution.

It is now clear that a moment of apparent *social* stability was only a brief moment on the long journey of the class called into being by the Industrial Revolution; a resting place in a prolonged period of global economic and political instability. The only constant in the story of class is that of perpetual

Mother Jones

Mary Harris Jones, 'Mother Jones' (1837-1930) was a prominent and effective US trade union activist. According to historian Daniel Guérin 'she was steeped in the democratic traditions which had shaped the US... When she summoned these traditions to her aid, putting to shame those who brazenly violated them... her opponents were at a loss for a reply to her accusations.'

She was imprisoned several times for her feisty acts of resistance. She would go kicking and screaming, with ringing words such as: 'If they want to hang me, let them. And on the scaffold I will shout "Freedom for the working class!"'

from Daniel Guérin, *100 Years of Labor History in the USA*, Ink Links 1979.

change; articulated memorably by Ma Joad at the end of John Steinbeck's classic novel of the US Depression, *The Grapes of Wrath*: everything changes; only the people go on.

Whatever material improvements, there is always insecurity and unchosen change with unpredictable social and moral costs. Organized labor had become complacent all over Europe; believing, perhaps, in its own invincibility, borrowing a luster of historic destiny from a Marxism which it spurned, but which still influenced any politics addressed to the constituency of labor. The people have always been perpetual economic migrants in landscapes not made by them, moving from one form of labor to another in response to technological innovation. Technology, undeniable though its benefits may be, has changed in a single direction, namely towards processes that increasingly dispensed with concentrations of workers, substituting mechanization, automation, robotization for human labor. This is carried out in the name of productivity; but it also disperses those required by labor-intensive industry, where their combined strength and power remain a constant threat to the owners of capital.

The end of 'class'...

Some academics, such as Peter Calvert[5], have suggested that the idea of class has outlived its usefulness. The complexity of modern society has effaced the antagonisms described by Marx; the word itself has little or no value, the indicators are unreliable. Others, such as sociologist Richard Scase[6], insist that in spite of this complexity the reality of the expansion of work functions (in selling, retailing and entertainment in the consumer society) does not alter the relationship between workers and those who profit from their labor.

It is certainly true that the common experience shared by the working class throughout Britain in its moment of stability has been fragmented in the last two generations, and replaced by a more individualistic ideology, a less coherent form of society. In this discussion, much hinges upon the idea of *class consciousness.*

There has been much political and academic argument over *objective* and *subjective* views of class. Marx insisted that whatever individuals may have thought about their class position, objective reality set proletarians against bourgeois: the interests of the owners of capital could not be reconciled with those they employed. The aim for Marx was to transform the class in itself into the class for itself, that is, to ensure the workers would develop consciousness of their position and act accordingly – they would become the agents of revolutionary social and economic transformation. He imagined that the most advanced capitalist countries would be the forerunners of what would be a global phenomenon.

The failure of these predictions in the Western countries led to much rationalization, and to some strange political contortions by Marxists and Marxist parties in the effort to explain why events had turned out in this way. The most common explanation was the idea of *false consciousness*: the inability of workers to acknowledge their true position and to behave appropriately. This led to various forms of conspiracy theory: the representatives and beneficiaries of capital have confused the working class so that they do not perceive where their real interests lie. Earlier, it was the capitalist propagandists, the manipulators of religious mythology (the promise of 'pie-in-the-sky').

...or the end of history?

But as the capitalist societies became more prosperous and delivered the goods, the villains changed. Now it was the capitalist media with their misrepresentation of reality which interfered with popular consciousness of the historic mission of the workers. The power of Marx's analysis is undiminished, although the consequences which he believed to be the inevitable outcome of that analysis have not occurred. If the world is unchanged in spite of everything having altered, this paradox is in considerable measure due to the dissonance between diagnosis and prognosis in Marx: from his ability to describe the way things *were*, he extrapolated the way they *must be*.

The Soviet State was established in the name of the working class. The subsequent distortions of its society, the violence, the lies and sacrifice of millions of human beings, ostensibly for the sake of socialism, are well known. The first leader, Lenin, created the basis for a new élite class, when he declared that the proletariat could not attain full consciousness without the aid of bourgeois intellectuals. In the Soviet Union, this task was entrusted to the Communist Party, which came to speak as though it, and not the people, was the proletariat. The terror of Lenin's successor Stalin, the slaughter of the Second World War and the incapacity of socialism to match the inventiveness of capitalism all led to the downfall of the Soviet Union. This created the faltering of belief and the crisis of faith in socialism. It is in the context of socialism's alleged 'unworkability', its contrariness to 'human nature' and its ideological simplicity, that capitalism has renewed itself globally with such dynamic vigor and energy.

The fate of the Soviet Union and the cruelty that forced human beings to live according to the dictates of ideology have been presented by the defenders of capitalism as evidence that Marx's analysis of class was false, that no politics can be grounded on his ideological premises. They have gone further. Taking their cue from the failure of communism they now maintain that capitalism expresses something profound and enduring about human relationships, that it is scarcely a system at all, but rather an emanation of the natural world itself. As a result, they say, we have reached 'the end of history'. But the story of class continues.

1 *The Making of the English Working Class*, EP Thompson, Pelican 1963. **2** *The Condition of the Working Class in England in 1844*, Friedrich Engels, George Allen and Unwin 1968. **3** *Languages of Class: Studies in English Working Class History 1832-1982*, Gareth Stedman Jones, Cambridge University Press 1982. **4** *A New View of Society*, Robert Owen, 1814, Penguin Classics 1991. **5** *The Concept of Class: An Historical Introduction*, Peter Calvert, Hutchinson 1982. **6** *Class*, Richard Scase, The Open University 1968.

3 Class: alive and kicking

How class relationships have been overtaken in the rich Western societies by a sense of inequality based on hierarchies of ethnic origin, gender and sexual orientation... and a look at the historical roots of this profound shift in popular sensibility.

THE CHANGES OF the past 50 years have imposed new layers of inequality. This process has been masked by the considerable material improvements that have taken place, a pattern which has affected all Western countries and Japan. There have been significant consequences for the accepted categories of class. While inequality – the distribution of wealth between rich and poor – in the 1990s bore a close resemblance to that of the 1890s, people's *subjective* experience has been of rising disposable income, transformation of living and working conditions unparalleled since the working class was born in the raw settlements of early industrialism.

At the root of present-day social stratification, the effects of the trauma of industrialization still remain: when the majority of the people, evicted from agrarian and rural society, became urban. Men, women and children were pressed into labor in mines, mills and factories often in degrading conditions, for prolonged periods of time, for wages barely at subsistence level. Such violence is not quickly overcome. Great wrongs never are – as the legacies of slavery, the Irish famine, the holocaust and the partition of India continue to show to the world.

Subsequent economic growth has not eliminated the scars of gross injustice imposed as Britain emerged as the industrial power-house of the world; scars visible in the variable life-expectancy between those born in affluent communities in the south of England and old inner-city populations of Glasgow or Liverpool, and in isolated pit villages. The same is seen in the US, where poor people in Washington DC or Appalachian mining communities produce statistics on child mortality more akin to those in the Third World than to their peers in California or Florida.

Shrinking working class

That older patterns persist, in spite of sustained economic improvements, is confirmed by many contemporary sources. Characteristic is a report in the UK *Guardian* on a government discussion-paper on social mobility: 'There is a strong association between class origins and class destination… The proportion of middle-class men who were socially "stable" did not change much during the 20th century. Figures show that most working-class children have working-class parents; ditto the offspring of people in professional or managerial positions.' The report concludes that mobility has grown as Britain has become a more middle-class society; but not in relative terms: 'Class continues to matter in the sense that the odds of a working-class child ending up middle class have not changed much over recent decades. What has happened is that the classes out of which people are not moving have shrunk.'[1] What this means can be expressed by simple statistics: in 1911, three-quarters of the jobs in the economy were manual labor; by 1951, two-thirds were manual; by 1991, only 37.7 per cent were manual. Professional and managerial employment grew from 7.5 per cent in 1911 to 33 per cent in 1991.

Onto this enduring pattern (albeit within a changing class composition of the population; a shrinking working class and growing middle class) inequality has grown within the UK, as in almost every other country in the world. This has coincided with the decay of the old industrial centers. If the phenomenal growth of industry traumatized those called into its service, the removal of that industry – to which people had over time accommodated themselves – was no less brutal. The old division of labor was swept away, the manufacturing and mining districts were left with the ruins of what had given them meaning. The social consequences in the big conurbations of Europe, the one-industry towns in the US and in the UK have been disastrous for the children of the former workers. Addictions to drugs and alcohol, the growth of crime, violence and family breakdown show themselves in the disadvantaging of a new generation.

New workers

The general rise in living standards of people in the West in the past 50 years has concealed increasing inequality. As poor people become less poor, they are less inclined to notice whether the well-off are becoming richer. Young people going into routine work in information technology or call centers, in marble-and-glass offices, in McDonald's or shopping malls like hanging gardens, look back on the laboring work of their parents and see what they themselves do as a significant advance.

This model of development has served to ease the changing division of labor, so that although the shock of the Industrial Revolution has been absent in *this* change, the consequences have been no less profound or far-reaching.

The erosion of *labor* in actually making material necessities was perceived as a positive process, since the change was associated with affluence. It is only later that some of the social costs of economic advance become visible. The absorption of many young people in low-paid service industries – catering, fast-food, retailing, hotel and security work, cleaning and domestic services – may suit those seeking to subsidize their studies or travel round the world, but when these become the *only* source of a full-time career, people find themselves trapped, confronted by the prospect of poorly rewarded labor, often casualized and with little security.

Indeed, in recent years we have seen the

Work in the services sector

In most regions, the employment of women and men is concentrated in the services sector (such as catering, working in shops, cleaning). Generally, women remain at the lower end of a segregated labor market and are concentrated in a few occupations, holding positions of little or no authority and receiving less pay than men.

Percentage distribution of the labor force, each sex, 1990/97

	Female labor force			Male labor force		
	Agriculture	Industry	Services	Agriculture	Industry	Services
Africa						
Northern Africa	30	21	48	17	31	52
Sub-Saharan Africa	65	7	28	57	16	27
Latin America & the Caribbean						
Caribbean	6	12	80	17	29	53
Central America	8	18	73	40	22	38
South America	5	13	81	12	31	56
Asia						
Eastern Asia	14	23	63	11	33	56
South-Eastern Asia	46	13	41	45	20	35
Southern Asia	66	18	15	54	13	32
Central Asia	42	14	43	39	24	34
Western Asia	21	16	63	17	33	50
Developed regions						
Eastern Europe	16	29	55	17	44	39
Western Europe	5	16	79	7	38	55
Other developed regions	3	13	84	6	31	64

The World's Women 2000, UN

reappearance of 'the laboring poor'. Although this is not a label used in the present day, the phenomenon is unmistakable. What looked like an archaic social idea has been reconstituted and scarcely mitigated by the existence of a (not always enforceable) minimum wage. Redistributive efforts by government can do little to match the lopsided rewards of a free market, which bestows its bounty with such spectacular unfairness.

Worldwide inequalities

Connected with this are the effects of a new global division of labor. The Western democracies are beneficiaries of a globalization which nevertheless exacerbates worldwide inequality. It also realigns the position of the people within one country in new forms of stratification. But since globalization represents the continuing dominance of the already rich countries, it has apparently advantaged a majority of the people in the US, Australia, Japan and other 'advanced' industrial countries. The radical reconfiguration of class in these countries means that a majority now identify with a global middle class, while the minority of poor have become an 'underclass'.

There is a further dimension in this re-working of class societies. The emergence into the labor market of large numbers of women; the presence in all the rich countries of people of other ethnicities, religions and countries – mostly migrants, in response to labor shortages at one time or another in the post-war era – has also added a conspicuous diversity to the working population.

In this, Europe has come to resemble the long-term pattern of migration into the US. The self-assertiveness of other groups – lesbians and gay men, people with disability, for instance – has also added to the diversity of the workforce. As a result, most contemporary discussion of equality has focused upon the relative access of these groups, formerly invisible or absent from the labor force, to the advantages enjoyed primarily by white middle-class males.

Establishing increased fairness among these may help equality of opportunity, a modest exercise in social justice, but it has an even greater advantage than this: it conceals the powerlessness of governments, international institutions or anyone else to remedy the great and growing divide between rich and poor in the world. A rearrangement of injustice in one country, so that all groups are more or less represented both in the advantaged and disadvantaged is an interesting experiment. It satisfies some of those excluded from the mainstream culture. But it leaves the wider structures of injustice untouched, or even stronger than they were, since those who gain from reforms are more likely to defend them against others seeking wider change – particularly when these others are the disenfranchised of the Third World.

Hierarchies today

This is not to diminish the importance of hierarchy within societies, any more than within social institutions and organizations. In the second half of the 20th century, as the importance of social class faded in the rich industrial societies, other patterns of belonging and identity emerged. These became the focus of profound realignments of people's sense of self.

The development of the women's movement, the growth of consciousness of blacks, Hispanics or Asians, the assertion of sexual orientation as defining characteristics, have all contributed to new forms of struggle for recognition and parity within society. In this process, class appeared secondary, although its salience remains undiminished, as we can now see, with the appearance of a black middle class and a lesbian and gay middle class. The work of these groups has been against discrimination, and in favor of equal access to employment and recognition. None has actually sought to overthrow the class relations of society, although the women's movement added a new radical dimension to the struggle. Insofar as women are seen as less competitive, more intuitive, more attuned to nurturing and tenderness than men, society may have been inflected by their concerns. However, industrial society has scarcely became more tender; although women gained in relation to men in terms of income in employment, they still lag behind by almost 20 per cent in wages for equivalent jobs.

As seen above, 'the 'politics of identity' in Western society replaced class in political and social struggles in the last decades of the 20th century. It is as though existential rather than social factors have become the main influences upon our sense of who we are. People

Working women

Women's share of the labor force has increased almost everywhere. In the UK, between 1911 and 1998, the number of women as a percentage of the workforce rose from 29.3 to 44.3. Women continue to earn less than men in all countries. For the period 1992/7: in Australia they earned 85% of men's wages; in Aotearoa/NZ 78%; in the UK 72%; in Bangladesh 50% and in Mexico 71%.

Percentage of the labor force who are women

	1980	1997		1980	1997
Africa			**Asia**		
Northern Africa	20	26	Eastern Asia	40	43
Sub-Saharan Africa	42	43	South-Eastern Asia	41	43
Southern Africa	40	40	Southern Asia	31	33
Rest of Sub-Saharan Africa	43	43	Central Asia	47	46
Latin America & the Caribbean			Western Asia	23	27
Caribbean	38	43	**Developed regions**		
Central America	27	33	Eastern Europe	45	45
South America	27	38	Western Europe	36	42
Oceania*	35	38	Other developed regions	39	44

* Sparse data for this subregion; average should be treated with caution

The World's Women 2000, UN

see themselves, not in terms of social function, but as a reflection of the most irreducible elements of their being – female, male, black, white, lesbian, gay or straight, young or old. Detachment from a Marxian obsession with the purely economic positioning of human beings in society is liberating; and the struggle for recognition responds to the more ample social and economic spaces within richer societies, so that for a majority survival is no longer the principal concern.

Resistance to sexism, racism and the acknowledgment of diversity in sexual orientation, however civilizing, are restricted to the enclaves of privilege which Western societies now are. This helps to ignore the fact that the great majority of the world's most exploited and humiliated people – those at the bottom of the global class-structure – are non-white women; while the plight of lesbians and gays in poor societies has scarcely yet begun to be discussed. The challenging of existential hierarchies in the countries of privilege is not a substitute for resistance against less easily eradicable, now global injustice. Women, blacks, lesbians and gay men, though, are identifiable human beings in ways that 'the unequal' are not.

Resistance in the US

It is no accident that as the Communist Party in the US fell apart in the 1950s, a new wave of resistance emerged. Starting with the bus boycott in Montgomery, Alabama, in 1955-6 led by Dr Martin Luther King Jr, escalating with the sit-in by black students in a number of Southern cities in 1960, it created a focus for change not based on class. The assassination of President Kennedy, the murder of Dr Martin Luther King Jr and opposition to the Vietnam War created a ferment of radicalism. This mutated however into groups which had been marginalized, excluded or discriminated against seeking a place within a society in which class had become only one determinant of disadvantage – and not, it seemed, the primary one – in the presence of the growing black consciousness, feminist, gay and lesbian movements of the subsequent decades.

All these factors must be borne in mind as we discuss the issue of class. Class isn't a matter of schematic changes: it is a story of how living flesh and

---

Reds under the bed

The relatively weak threat of socialism in the United States did not lead to greater tolerance in the period following the Second World War. The Communist Party in the US never had more than 100,000 members (out of a population at the time of c110 million), but during the early years of the Cold War, any form of radicalism was suspect, and Communists came under particular attack. By the mid-1950s, many Party leaders had been imprisoned, while thousands of members had appeared before Congressional committees, had been refused passports, and deprived of livelihood. The anti-Communist hysteria in the US was a curious parallel to the Stalinism against which it was engendered. ■

blood experience the injuries and humiliations, how they justify privilege and resist oppression within the hierarchies and orders of society.

Faceless statistics

All the contemporary data on wealth and poverty consist of facts and figures, which merely state the existing situation. There is nothing in such data to suggest how such a state of affairs came about, even less about what might be done to change it. They remain detached from the people they refer to. It is perhaps not by chance that the UN agencies, the World Bank, the International Monetary Fund (IMF) and all overseas aid programs of Western governments are committed to strategies for 'poverty abatement', to 'halve the numbers in poverty by 2015'. The crusade is against 'poverty', an abstraction; references to 'the poor' do little more to rescue humanity from this abstraction. And with good reason.

We have seen how the idea of class has given way to the notion of *inequality*. This is a far more impersonal formulation than class resentment, which used to be maligned as the 'politics of envy'. An apparently innocent shift covers a profound psychological change in perceptions of social injustice.

The war between classes has sunk out of sight, and instead, we see a continuum of haves and have-nots. This can be presented as a purely administrative problem, to be tackled by experts, governments and international agencies. The advantage of class identity and recognition of the clash of interests was that this was open to political remedy. You could identify those who flaunted their wealth in the face of prevailing poverty. People could take action by electing governments who would address their grievances. If this failed, they could confront their expropriators. 'Inequality' gives no sense of belonging to any group that can act collectively. *Unequal* is what individuals are; *class* is what you belong to if you want to mobilize for some reform or improvement. Those who rejoice over the decline in 'sterile' class conflict are celebrating the loss of any practical redress open to the people themselves. The abstraction of 'inequality' forestalls autonomous popular action. There are no actors in 'inequality'.

When the victims of inequality – as opposed to the members of a lower or subordinate class – look at the world around them, they see only other individuals. This is why they compare their position with those of neighbors, fellow-workers, friends and acquaintances; and seek *personal* advancement in relation to individuals rather than *social* advancement in terms of groups. The impotence of individuals has displaced the potential power of organized groups – a fact which no doubt has given rise to all the rhetoric of 'empowerment', 'inclusion' and 'participation'; those adornments of a widely felt powerlessness.

In the academic neutrality of graphs and tables of inequality, we may wonder how the people came to lose consciousness; particularly since education, information, knowledge, facts and all the other paraphernalia of communication are now the object of multi-billion dollar conglomerates and empires that bestride the globe. Whatever the purpose of all these agents of instruction, it is clear that the creation of resistance to the progress of inequality is not among them.

'Data, data everywhere and not a thought to think'

The abundance of information about the world seems to spread incoherence rather than understanding, at least on this one central point. This has been reinforced by the idea of globalization – something so awesome that people fall silent in its presence, as though it were the will of God. In fact, globalization is an ideology: it represents the expansion of capitalism throughout the world. As such, far from being a new phenomenon, it plays out on an even grander scale what happened within Britain and other industrializing countries almost two centuries ago.

We have been here before. In the years of driven upheaval that turned Britain from an agrarian into an industrial society, an impoverished peasantry was coerced into a quite alien way of life. They were unfamiliar with the forces shaping their lives. They forsook the villages and the countryside, where they had lived as agricultural laborers, smallholders, servants and artisans. As they entered into factories, mills and mines, a new kind of human being was fashioned by mass manufacture. The tormenting consequences of this process were clear. In the 1780s, there were around 40 lunatic asylums in England and Wales; 60 years later, there were 400. Similarly, today, in the cities of the Third World, you don't have to look far for signs of mental disorder in an uprooted, disoriented peasantry. I recall a startling image from Manila, in the Philippines. On the Payatas garbage-dump, hundreds of people were moving back and forth over the steaming garbage, turning over the debris, in a crude mimicry of the agriculture from which they had been recently evicted.

If laborers in the early industrial period in Britain were left to the economic effects of *laissez-faire* (belief in the sanctity of free markets, with which governments interfered at their peril – a dogma now borne by the structural adjustment programs of the IMF), the poor by contrast were under constant scrutiny by government. They became the object of punitive legislation. The Royal Commission on the Poor Laws Report, which led to the Poor Law Amendment Act of 1834, stated that 'every penny bestowed, that tends to render the condition of the pauper more eligible than that of the independent laborer, is a bounty on indolence and vice'.

This found expression in the law of less eligibility, the aim of which was to make the condition of the best-off person in the workhouse worse than that of the most ill-paid laborer outside. The workhouse became a symbolic building in every town and city in Britain. Generations of working people lived in dread of ending their days inside its bleak forbidding walls.

The 'gravediggers of capitalism'

As we have seen, people formed by and within the new industrial society learned a great deal as time went by. The confusion slowly cleared, and people employed in industry began to discern patterns behind their poverty. As historian Eric Hobsbawm said, 'the working class spent the first half of the 19th century at the mercy of capital, and the second half learning the rules of the game'. EP Thompson referred to the transformation of the 18th century mob into 'a revolutionary crowd' by their experience of industrialism. The working class is both subject and object in the story of industrialism. Although a factor of production (labor), the living flesh and blood behind this abstraction are also conscious, thinking individuals, who make sense of the forces that control their lives, and find ways of coping with them. Sometimes this means building defenses, sometimes trying to shape those forces towards more humane ends.

This suggests the birth of *consciousness*, the sense of a shared predicament. It was not a difficult lesson, that the relationship of the workers to capital was constant, and that improvements in living standards could be achieved only collectively. Whatever the various strands of political and economic thought propounded by economists and intellectuals, it became clear that the only effective response to the systemic violence and insecurity of their condition was some form of collective organization. This expressed itself, first in trade unionism, and later, in political parties.

If class in industrial society was defined by Marx as an expression of the relationship between people to the means of production, this has subsequently proved an incomplete formulation. The efforts of academics, ideologists and apologists of capitalism to show its inadequacy have been both ingenious and fruitful; but all their efforts were unable to diminish the majestic power Marx assumed over the imagination of intellectuals and revolutionaries all over the world. Discussions of class for more than a century and a half were preoccupied with the condition of the working classes; not least because of Marx's terrifying prediction that they would become 'the gravediggers of capitalism'[2].

Concern with the working class eclipsed earlier class conflict. In the early 19th century there was considerable enmity between the old landed aristocratic order and the emerging middle class, entrepreneurs and manufacturers, the *nouveaux-riches* makers of fortunes. These were viewed with suspicion by the old order, the landed interests of aristocracy and gentry, who had been the conservers of privilege and the upholders of a system of semi-feudal hierarchies.

The rise of the middle class or bourgeoisie

This growing middle class alarmed ruling élites with its lack of respect for tradition and the honor due to power and privilege. An energetic, resourceful middle class allied itself with the turbulent, unpredictable working class in the agitation to reform the franchise, which would give *them* power, but deny it to the workers. This culminated in the Reform Bill of 1832.

The most resounding paean of praise to the energies of the new middle class is found in Marx and Engels' *Manifesto of the Communist Party* (published in 1848, but in English only in 1869)[2]. This may seem an unlikely place to look for commendations of capitalism. Paradoxically, the power and energy of capital which Marx and Engels acknowledged, also presaged the disintegration of the alternative – socialism (which had not even come into being at that time).

They wrote: 'The *bourgeoisie*, wherever it has got the upper hand, has put an end to all feudal, patriarchal, idyllic relations. It has pitilessly torn asunder the motley feudal ties that bound man [sic] to his 'natural superiors', and has left remaining no other nexus between man and man than naked self-interest, than callous 'cash-payment'... [The bourgeoisie] has been the first to show what man's [sic] activity can bring about. It has accomplished wonders far surpassing Egyptian pyramids, Roman aqueducts, and Gothic cathedrals; it has conducted expeditions that put in the shade all former Exoduses and crusades... Constant revolutionizing of production, uninterrupted disturbance of all social conditions, everlasting uncertainty and agitation distinguish the bourgeois epoch from all earlier ones. All fixed, fast-frozen relations, with their train of ancient and venerable prejudices and opinions, are swept away, all new-formed ones become antiquated before they can ossify. All that is solid melts into air, all that is holy is profaned, and man is at last compelled to face, with sober senses, his real conditions of life and his relations with his kind.'

With testimonials like this, one might have thought, the bourgeoisie was in for a long stay. And so it has proved.

In allowing the middle class the vote, the Reform Bill of 1832 mollified any dangerous political radicalism they might have entertained. The fears of the ruling class were allayed by their own capacity to absorb those they regarded as vulgar upstarts. In any case, they were also impressed by the ingenuity and wealth-making power of the new class.

It became the aim of the new rich to educate and bring up their children in imitation of the landed families, with whom they contracted judicious marriages, ensuring the perpetuation of privilege, and its extension to those who had transformed the country. Martin Wiener in *English Culture and the*

Decline of the Industrial Spirit 1850-1980, writes of 'the gentrification of the industrialist'. He says 'social prestige and moral approbation were to be found using the wealth acquired in industry to escape it... As a rule, leaders of commerce and industry in England over the past century have accommodated themselves to an élite culture blended of pre-industrial aristocratic and religious values and more recent professional and bureaucratic values that inhibited their quest for expansionism, productivity and profit'.

Social critic Raymond Williams came to a similar conclusion, from a different standpoint, when he wrote in *The Long Revolution* that 'somewhere in the 19th century (though there are earlier signs) the English middle class lost its nerve, socially, and thoroughly compromised with the class it had virtually defeated' [ie the landed, aristocratic class]. This compromise prefigured an even more momentous compromise later, between capital and labor.

What about the workers?

Whatever antagonisms persisted between older élites and the class of industrialists in the 19th century, these were overshadowed by the question of taming the laboring poor. The publication in 1867 of Marx's *Das Kapital* ('Capital') left Britain untouched. Alarm over his prediction that the growing impoverishment of those with nothing but their labor-power to sell, the coming revolution, the dictatorship of the proletariat and eventual coming about of socialism scarcely dented the glory of the high moment of imperial ascendancy, even though discussions about the laboring poor had haunted politics in Britain in the preceding half century. Much of the evidence on which Marx relied had been gathered in Britain.

Discussions of class relationships often come limping behind the actual reality. The data for *Das Kapital* were gathered earlier in the century. Its publication coincided with the long mid-Victorian period of prosperity which, nourished in considerable part by the wealth Britain gained from its colonial possessions, saw a significant advance by the working class. *Das Kapital* did not appear in England until 1887. This coincided with a new period of economic turbulence and social unrest. Social observers, reformers and critics had been publishing lurid accounts of the poor throughout the century; no one really knew just how dangerous and threatening the laboring poor might be, should they unite against the propertied classes.

The extension of the franchise in 1867 to (male) householders, suggested that recruitment to the middle class was a continuous process. For the first time, it appeared that a significant proportion of the working class might also be accommodated within a system from which it once seemed they would remain permanently estranged. Many far-sighted defenders of capitalism foresaw that a system which had absorbed the middle class might also be flexible enough to swallow the working class too; although, to become really effective, this had to wait until the second half of the 20th century.

War and ferment

This was no smooth and easy operation. The militancy of the labor movement in the years before the First World War, and the carnage of that conflict, interrupted the process of assimilation, as did the Depression. The 60 years between 1871 and 1931 saw a net loss through emigration of two million people from England and Wales alone; many the most active and energetic. Without the safety valve of migration, it would have been more difficult to contain the restiveness of the time.

The Russian Revolution of 1917 gave new urgency to the issue of the working class. This event scarred the consciousness of ruling élites all over the world and served as a warning of what might happen if they neglected the welfare of the working class. Even so, the ideology of Marxism had greater influence upon intellectuals than upon the workers.

A second trauma to the ruling classes occurred with the rise of Nazism and Fascism in Europe. This was an age of extremes, when Left and Right battled over ideological ownership of the 'masses', as the working class were still then called. The ideology of racism, which had animated its imperial adventures, was repatriated to Europe by Nazism. The only alternative seemed the horrors of Stalinism. The alliance of the Western democracies with the Soviet Union in the defeat of Hitler was broken after the Second World War and Soviet Russia annexed large parts of Eastern Europe.

These convulsions clearly required a more imaginative response. With Europe in ruins, the opening up of the concentration camps, the A-bombs on Hiroshima and Nagasaki which ended the war in Japan, it seemed there could be no question of resuming business as usual in Europe.

This was the time of the 'post-war settlement' between capital and labor. The war had touched people as never before, since it had been brought to civilian populations by bombing from the war in the air. 1945 did indeed mark a radical moment and the victory over Nazism seemed to mark a decisive break with the past. It looked as though accommodation might be possible between what had been seen as incompatible interests.

The post-war world

In the Western world, the welfare state in its various forms was the pledge that concern for the poor, the disadvantaged and excluded would ensure 'cradle to grave' health care, protection for disability, sickness and unemployment, with pensions for the elderly guaranteed by the state. This appeared to be a permanent arrangement, whereby social peace would be assured. The working class would be comfortably installed within industrial society. The government would protect the least defended and moderate the grossest injustices of capitalism, while not inhibiting the creation of wealth. In Britain, many of the practical virtues of working-class life, particularly those undertaken by women and the care and protection of the needy, were enshrined in legislation. The welfare state promised liberation; and was, for many, a vindication of the years of struggle.

This compromise worked for a generation after the Second World War – a time of reconstruction, economic expansion and growth without precedent. Inspired by the mass consumer society pioneered by the US, goods and services which had been denied to the majority became available in great abundance. But the ideological struggle between capital and labor, which seemed to have been laid to rest in the consensus of 1945, did not go away. It became a kind of underground guerrilla warfare. Free-market economist FA von Hayek's *The Road to Serfdom*[3], a denunciation of socialism and the state, laid the ground for the market counter-offensive.

The response by capital to the public provision of the welfare state was a rehabilitation of the free market, which led to the explosion of material goods, and gave rise to what liberal economist JK Galbraith[4] called in 1958 'the affluent society' and later came to be recognized as a 'consumer society'. The triumphant comeback of the market and the undermining of collective action began in the 1950s. It took half a century to play itself out and to manifest itself in the harsh necessities of globalization, with fateful results for social class, both within countries and between countries.

It might have been – but wasn't – foreseen. Nothing lasts in human affairs, least of all in the inventive and opportunistic system of capitalism. The comfortable arrangement of the post-war world was destined to be swept away by events, consequences of which we will return to presently.

Galbraith identified the issue of the receding importance of social injustice as early as 1958. He wrote: 'The decline in concern for inequality cannot be explained by the triumph of equality. Although this is regularly suggested in the conventional wisdom of conservatives, and could readily be inferred from the complaints of businessmen, inequality is still great. In 1970, the one-tenth of families and unattached individuals with the lowest incomes received before taxes about 2 per cent of the total money income of the country; the tenth with the highest incomes received 27 per cent of the total, which is to say, their incomes averaged 14 times as much of the lowest tenth.' (The figures for 1999 show 1.8 per cent going to the bottom 10 per cent and 30.5 to the top 10 per cent.)

Galbraith continued: 'In the advanced countries, increased production is an alternative to redistribution… It has been the greatest solvent of the tension associated with inequality. Even though the latter persists, the awkward conflict which its correction implies can be avoided.' By this means, 'the oldest and most agitated of social issues, if not solved, is at least largely in abeyance, and the disputants have concentrated their attention, instead, on the goal of increased productivity'. The 'disputants' in this elegant euphemism are more familiar to us as the working class and the middle and upper classes.

The level playing field

The great advantage to governments and bureaucracies in the substitution of 'inequality' for 'class conflict' is that remedies for inequality appear more in their control than redress for the amorphous, more menacing gulfs between classes. Inequality is a subject to be studied in the hush of academic common-rooms and expressed in the high moral tone of political manifestos. Since equality is considered neither feasible nor desirable, equality of opportunity has been substituted; in the jargon, the 'level playing-field', that will enable the school drop-out kids of the long-term unemployed parents on the public housing scheme to compete with the child of the stockbroker and company executive from the mansion in Bel Air or Houston, so that the 'outcome' of their lives will not diverge dramatically.

Equality of opportunity is as far as a system of institutionalized class difference can go in redressing these matters. That it is largely a polite fiction goes without saying. There are several objections. Not least is that of the example cited above. Vast inherited differentials of wealth are matched by the ability to play the system successfully. The articulate and competent know how to gain all the advantages their society provides for them and their children; while those born to the pain of struggle at the bottom of a market-dominated society cannot possibly be compensated by any conceivable state – or private – provision for their disadvantage.

But the second objection is more telling. Profound inequalities are characteristics of any human society, in terms of motivation and commitment, as well as the even more significant factors of endowment, character and temperament. For many years I worked with children designated by society at that time as 'educationally subnormal'. They went to sheltered schools until they were 16, after which they were sent to make their accommodation with the world. That many found their way into the criminal justice system, others became homeless, while some held on to the most ill-paid and exploitative work, did nothing to impair society's absolute commitment to competitive principles. Yet they were destined to failure; and without their serene compliance with this fate, success would never be able to parade itself with its customary pride and self-satisfaction.

Why should those disadvantaged by nature, by

inheritance, by misfortune be cast as the shadow of the enterprising, the clever and the cunning? There is as strong a moral argument in favor of compensating such people as there is for sweeping them up in ideological battles which assign merit on the basis of qualities they do not possess.

Natural inequalities are one thing, but when these are set against constant social and economic flux, they are greatly exacerbated, as we shall see in the next chapter.

1 *The Guardian*, 30 April 2001. **2** *Manifesto of the Communist Party*, K Marx and F Engels, Progress Publishers 1977. **3** *The Road to Serfdom*, FA von Hayek, University of Chicago Press 1944. **4** *The Affluent Society*, JK Galbraith, Penguin 1982.

4 The consistency of change

How change has always characterized industrial society... and how classes are constantly made and re-made... The effects of globalization on class... and how this is reconstituting national class structures in a wider integrated system.

THE ONLY CONSTANT element in industrial society is perpetual *change*. This is often taken to mean technological change, although the application of evolving technologies also has a profound impact upon the psyche and character of people. Indeed, if we want to understand the development of industrial society, we need to look closely at how technology alters the sensibility of the people.

Broadly, (and if we discount the 1.5 million domestic servants, who in Britain made up the largest single category of employed persons until 1914), it can be said that in the mid-18th century twice as many people were involved in agriculture as in manufacture. By the 1840s, this proportion had been reversed, so that there were more than twice as many in manufacture as in the rural economy. It is impossible to overstate what migration from rural to urban society meant for those affected by it. It involved the dismantling of a human personality, shaped by the changing seasons, by seed-time and harvest, by the ceremonies, festivals and rituals of the country calendar. It created a new kind of human being formed by, within and for industrial society. Detached from the rhythm of the seasons, they had to adapt to the seasons of money – the daily or weekly wage, to dependence upon an income to provide all necessities. Country people had traditionally gathered firewood, grazed animals, picked wild fruits and nuts, caught rabbits and birds, plucked medicinal herbs and plants and had grown vegetables on small garden plots. They had eked out a living from common land and private woods and fields, even though landlords protected themselves against poaching. This was impossible in streets and slums where the industrial population lived. New habits of discipline were required, including regimented behavior so people were at work by the time the machinery started up.

Many pre-industrial manufacturing occupations – notably handloom weavers – had combined work at home (in which all members of the family participated, including children) with subsistence, maintaining a pig and a garden. They valued their independence. In the early part of the 19th century, they were starved out of livelihood by the growth of the factory system and reluctantly they passed their children over to the new factories. After the Napoleonic Wars, historian EP Thompson states, 'weaving, next to general laboring, was the grand resource of the northern unemployed. Fustian weaving was heavy, monotonous, but easily learned. Agricultural workers, demobilized soldiers, Irish immigrants – all continued to swell the labor force.'

Thompson asserts 'the artisan *felt* that his [sic] status and standard of living were under threat or were deteriorating between 1815 and 1840. Technical innovation and the abundance of cheap labor weakened his position. He had no political rights and the power of the State was used, if only fitfully, to destroy his trade unions'. Whatever evidence economists may have used to demonstrate that incomes rose during the early industrial period, Thompson points out this could not compensate for serious losses – of status, of freedom, of traditional life-ways – which cannot be adequately measured by purely economic instruments.

This important argument – the issue of economic improvement in relation to non-economic social, cultural and spiritual losses – has underlain much discussion about industrial society, but it has always remained subordinate. In our time the social and moral costs of capitalism have taken on new significance (the prevalence of crime, drugs, addictions, breakdown of human associations in the 'advanced' capitalist countries) – but especially in relation to the environment. The question now is also whether the resource-base of the planet can bear the intensive industrialization of the whole world, and whether the sacrifice of non-economic satisfactions (in this case, survival itself!) is too high a price to pay for the benefits humanity expects from more of the same. This issue is at the heart of new ideological struggles that have, in some ways, supplanted class struggle, and in others, extended it.

Perpetual insecurity

The capitalist system destroyed traditional ways of answering need, and made perpetual insecurity part of the life of those who had only their labor-power to bargain with. We can now survey 200 years of industrialization, and see that from time to time people have resisted the imposition of new technologies, particularly when these destroy livelihoods. The Luddites in Britain in the early 19th century smashed machinery they saw as degrading their skills and robbing them of their labor. So profound was the effect of this, that the word has remained in the vocabulary, usually as a term of abuse against anyone who stands in the path of 'progress'; and progress, in this sense, almost invariably means the appropriation of work by machinery of one kind or another. To call people 'Luddites' is to see them as wreckers of the well-being of the people, since it is axiomatic that technological advances go hand-in-hand with improvements in their lives.

There have been moments of stability in industrial society, even of apparent security. At least, once established, it seemed *comprehensible*. By the mid-19th century, in the division of labor in Britain, almost every place was associated with the production of some necessary object of daily life. It seemed for example that Lancashire would 'always' be associated with cotton goods, Yorkshire with woolens. Sheffield meant the steel industry, the manufacture of cutlery and household metal goods.

The contrast with the experience of the US could not be more dramatic, although some cities did become closely associated with their manufactures (Pittsburg and steel, Detroit and cars for example). It seems that the migratory spirit entered into the psyche of the people in the US, with their greater mobility and readiness to adapt to changing circumstances. The great waves that moved westwards, shifting out of one occupation into another, changing their environment and livelihood in response to conditions, did so in a quite different spirit from that which drove people in Britain into industrial society. The sense of space in the US, the possibility of leaving behind ruined places – whether dust bowl or rust belt – were not available in Britain.

In Britain, unlike in the US, the moment of industrial stability created the impression, for those who lived through it, of a lasting structure – as though the working class that then lived in the streets of the industrial towns represented *the* working class: a more or less settled state, destined to remain the same, serving local factories, mills and mines throughout the country.

It may seem extraordinary in retrospect that two or three generations were enough to give a sense of rootedness and permanence. But this conviction formed the basis for a whole literature and much academic research, which intensified the closer it came to dissolution. In the post-war period, there was an explosion of plays, films, TV and radio programs about the working class. Voices that had never before been 'officially' heard publicly became fashionable. It seemed in the 1960s that the working class had at last been liberated from imprisoning and deterministic patterns of work. Parents declared heroically 'no son of mine is going into the pits', as the pits were closing all around them. They had earlier vowed their daughters would not go into domestic service, at the time when the early gadgets of proto-consumerism were making maids-of-all-work a redundant luxury in the houses of the rich.

Roots of radicalism

Political radicalism was also believed to be a constant in the working class. In part this reflects the circumstances in which the working class came into existence. Amid terrible brutality, social injustice and squalor, what EP Thompson called 'the making of the English working class' created a life apart from that of their social superiors: they lived in an industrial apartheid. Thompson subscribed to the view that the making of the class also involved a sense of its own self-consciousness, a growing awareness which it would use to change the terms and conditions of its own existence.

The great epic of socialism was built upon the radical or revolutionary position of labor in relation to capital. This can now be seen to have been illusory. The transformation that has occurred in our time gives the lie to the idea of an inherently *radical* working class. Indeed, it is circumstances that determine whether it is the conservative or the radical element in people which will dominate politics at any time and no class has a monopoly of either radicalism or conservatism.

What is now called 'globalization' (present in embryo ever since the great global piratical incursions of Europeans into other cultures all over the world) dismantled the structures of belonging and identity which seemed so enduring in the 'classic' late-Victorian/early 20th-century working class.

Yet another profound shift in the sensibility of the people has characterized the period from the 1950s to the new century. This corresponds to structural change in the occupations of the people, and echoes the great epic of transformation in the move from agriculture to industry during the Industrial Revolution. Only this time it is the numbers of people in manufacturing that have been more or less halved, while the proportion in services – including health, social services, tourism and catering, finance and banking – has doubled. Such a dramatic alteration in the employment of people has significant repercussions upon their sense of identity, their social and economic purposes.

In the past 50 years, there has been a similar feeling of upheaval and the epochal transformation which distinguished the early industrial era. The presence of people from other parts of the world – initially migrants brought to service an economy of full employment, but later with a momentum of its own. The new assertiveness and altered awareness of women demanding fuller participation in economic and social life, the self-confidence of alternative sexualities, have all contributed to the decay of what had earlier been seen as the embodiment of a 'classic' working class.

But a question hovers over this new diverse, pluralist working class. The old occupations, with their discipline and sameness, the world of apprenticeships, initiations into patterns of work, the leisure culture of soccer and pubs, were based upon the manufacture of demonstrable necessities, from the nails and rivets, to the bicycles and ships. How is it that a whole class can be more or less released from the making of such indispensable objects of daily consumption as shoes and clothing, the utensils for living? How can a society abandon the production of items essential for its survival?

Global factories

This brings us to the new, global division of labor, whereby goods formerly made locally now arrive in the shops from distant, often unknown, origins in other parts of the world. Over the past 30 years in most Western industrial countries, whole industries have been wiped out, often those thought to have been the very basis of our wealth. People watched as factories that had stood for 150 years crashed in a tangle of rusty iron and brick-dust. They walked around department stores, picking up shoes and garments from Brazil or Taiwan, convinced they would fall apart when they put them on.

The shock of that loss was never recognized by our leaders. The pain of giving up the making of useful things was not acknowledged by the eager apologists of globalization, any more than the extinction of communities which had grown around coal or steel or fabrics, and which were so swiftly replaced by people divided by drugs, drink and other addictions, by the rupture of ties of kin, the dispersal of neighbors and breakdown of belonging.

Of course, people grew richer. There was more money about. They could afford new things to replace the durable serviceable objects now commanding high prices in the thrift shops of the area; but the intangible losses were never even discussed. If anyone even alluded to such a possibility she or he was accused of living in the past, indulging in nostalgia, wanting to go back to a mythic golden age – even though, whatever ages the working class may have endured, there was never yet one of precious metal.

Change and loss have been a continuous part of the life of the people, even when gains were at their most gaudy and conspicuous. Cars and holidays abroad were very fine things; but they did not supply a sense of purpose to those evicted from known and familiar patterns of employment. Again, the constant element is insecurity. Many people found their world threatened when their houses were demolished, declared unfit for habitation, their children departed for a career in London or abroad, and the networks of kinship that had sustained them in adversity dissolved in the corrosive acid of a busy individualism.

The urgency of change has accelerated since the dismantling of the division of labor within one country. Perhaps this is why the economy that replaced the familiar landscape brings so much stress, anxiety, strains relationships to breaking point, imposes new forms of ill-being and dis-ease unfamiliar to those who spent the last years of their lives coughing from asbestos dust or silicosis, or as victims of the mercilessly marketed lethal pleasures of the poor, cigarettes or alcohol. Certainly it has brought undreamed-of forms of labor to people, an expanding universe of work and opportunity. In the UK census of 1851, 7,000 occupations were listed. By 1881, this had increased to 12,000. The census of 1981 recorded 23,000.

Class and the wider world

The spaces emptied of the necessary labor of the working class have not remained unoccupied. The new division of labor, being less concerned with the stern materialities, also leaves room for a luxuriance of *fantasy*; so that human livelihoods cease to be the main – or even a principal – determinant on identity. Other factors dominate our sense of self.

What people consume has become a more immediate aspect of identity than what they do, make or create. This accounts for both the dissolution of the old working class, and the reconstitution of the psyche of the people in the image of the market. Consumer markets now exercise a major influence upon children and hence, upon the adults they become. Indeed, an older working class culture melted away very swiftly in the presence of new consumer freedoms. Only these, too – like every other aspect of our lives – have long-term effects not easily foreseen. It is an old story. It is easy to know what we are liberated *from*; but liberation also has a destination, which, in the moment of emancipation, is rarely visible. Our eyes remain fixed upon the past from which we have been released, and we do not look where we are heading; partly because it is unknown, but partly because arrival is rarely at the place anticipated.

The basic needs of society do not, of course, become dispensable with growing prosperity. These still have to be produced somewhere.

And while the people exult in new-found freedoms, all over the world new populations are being conjured out of a wasting peasantry, out of dispossessed country people, out of the landless, out of those evicted from homestead and farm. They create a vast procession of humanity, moving out of an impoverished rural and agrarian culture, towards the growing cities – just as occurred in Britain in the first half of the 19th century.

The places to which they migrate bear an uncanny resemblance to the scenes of exploitation and impoverishment which poor, hungry people discovered in 19th-century Chicago, Toronto or Manchester. Not surprisingly, once there, the occupations they find are often precisely those relinquished by our own 'liberated' peoples.

The destiny of the Western working class cannot be separated from the wider world. In fact, it never could. The wealth flowing into Britain from the Empire helped raise the living standards of even the laboring poor. The living conditions of the early industrial workers were squalid and degrading, and the small comforts which accrued to them as the century advanced played their part in maintaining relative social peace. Many of these came from territories ruled from Britain. Tea, tobacco and snuff, coffee, chocolate, sugar, cloves and cinnamon, rice (used for puddings) nutmeg, the laudanum (a derivative of opium) with which they pacified their children, and occasionally committed suicide; later, canned goods, pineapples and peaches, corned beef – the story of the

19th century is also one of people whose poverty was alleviated by tropical products, made possible by the cheapness of their extraction. This was a foretaste of global consumerism, which now places at the disposal of people luxuries from all over the world.

The load of toil

Because the burdens of industrialism fell disproportionately upon the workers, it became the ambition of reformers, visionaries and socialists to diminish that heavy load of toil. Some – such as socialist William Morris[1] – pointed out late in the 19th century that the moment had passed where excessive labor was vital to the provision of necessities. He denounced the 'world market' which privileged the whims of the rich over the needs of the poor. It has since become even more apparent that the 'work-ethic' has become irrelevant in a world where automation, robotics and *jidoka* (the manipulation of artificial intelligence) are routinely applied to production. The pain and effort with which discipline was imposed on the workers created the heroic myth of labor.

It is now widely acknowledged that liberation from debilitating work is both feasible and desirable. It is obvious that there is no longer any need for profoundly oppressive and exploitative labor in the world. But it would be a disaster for the capitalist system to recognize this, since it is founded on the inevitability of a labor without end. So the myth has to be maintained that work, work and more work is required; the way this is done is to tether people to the idea that only by excessive labor will they be able to buy all the glittering goods held out before them.

Philosopher André Gorz wrote that 'what is happening is that industrial society is doing its best to hide the fact that the amount of socially necessary labor is declining rapidly and that everyone could benefit from this'[2]. Such a systemic catastrophe has to be avoided; and one way in which this has occurred has been the rise of what we may call a *consumeriat*, almost a mirror-image of Marx's proletariat, which makes people submit to any intensification of labor for the money that will procure the goods and services essential for a full life. There has also been an appropriation by the privileged of the heroic role of labor. This corresponds to an ever more elaborate division of labor in capitalism, a process which makes more opaque the relationship between the owners of capital and workers. The growth of service industries, leisure, tourism, entertainment, retailing and travel adds a new dimension to the vast expansion of technical personnel, scientists, designers and other functionaries, who enrich the global system with their talents. In this way, executives, high-flying commercial and industrial personnel, celebrities and pop-stars, workers in the media, advertising and publicity, academics and researchers – the martyrized victims of fame immolated to an adoring public – have assumed the mantle of indispensable labor, which was formerly the consolation of workers in factories, mines and mills. These people are constantly seen on TV, talking about their arduous schedules, their commitment to grandiose projects, their coast-to-coast appearances, the demands of their fans, their bruising and life-threatening high-energy movements, their high-octane endeavors which leave them exhausted and in need of expensive recuperation.

Work and jobs

In this way, even the consolation of the working class – work – has been taken away from them, just as their old cottages have been turned into weekend homes, and the tenements in which they lived in squalor, the factories in which they toiled and the warehouses in which the goods they made were stored, have been refurbished for the benefit of a metropolitan élite. In *The Leisure Society*[3] I wrote: 'We have only to consider all the voluntary 'workaholics' in our society... The commitment to work may be seen in the conspicuous 'punishing schedules' of business people, the commuters of transnational corporations whose budgetary responsibilities are said to exceed those of many sizable nation-states, in the ills attendant upon the series of identical luxury hotels, the jet-lag and hangovers from the unavoidable hospitality which is part of their duty of selling British, showing the flag, boosting exports, chasing up orders, opening up markets, clocking up sales. Their weary attendance at expensive restaurants where so much vital work is done; the obligatory nights in the opera boxes which their company reserves for the season; the entertainment of irksome foreign buyers on their yacht or in their mansion behind the screens of shrubs... the indulgence of the whims of potential customers on the rain-swept golf courses or in discreet and expensive sex parlors; the vast expenditure of energy in the futures, commodity and stock markets which burn people out before they reach 35 – all this amounts to an oppressive excess of labor, a sacrifice to command the awe and compassion of those called to perform no such exalted task in the world.'

A working class whose labor has been taken over by that of their social 'superiors' has a severely diminished claim to recognition. Work is now what the élite do, and jobs are what the workers have; a change in the use of a monosyllable covers an epic shift in both the social and, by implication, the moral designation of whole classes of people.

This marks an interesting reversal of what Thorstein Veblen – one of the few American writers to have been preoccupied with class in the early years of the 20th century – described in his *Theory of the Leisure Class*[4]. At that time, Veblen saw the rich – the leisure class – as under the necessity of distancing itself as far as possible from necessary labor, and advertising its conspicuous consumption. What a contrast in an age of mass conspicuous consumption, that the rich should feel obliged to advertise its central importance and functional usefulness!

The reconstitution of the working class

The decay of the national division of labor in the countries of Europe could not have occurred unless it had been reconstituted at a global level (or semi-global, as long as the Soviet Union still existed: the presence of an alternative economic system for a long time prevented incursions by capitalism in what used to be called The Second World). Since 1990 this has no longer been a factor, and little has checked the growth of globalization – an apparently neutral term, which means the worldwide dominance of capitalism. This is sometimes called the free market system; although it is plain that while money moves freely around the world, goods are occasionally restricted and the movement of labor is rigorously controlled.

Generally, the dissolution of the working class in Britain or France or Australia has been seen in isolation from globalization, which has been a major factor in the process. As the countries of the world become more interdependent (but also more unequal), it seems the politics of individual countries become more parochial. One result of this has been that the making of a *global* working class has been obscured by the noisy celebration of the end of the most virulent class antagonisms in the rich world. These remain, but as irritants rather than as major social conflicts.

The significance of a global division of labor in a single economic system is rarely spelt out. It is too disturbing. The majority of the people in the G-8 richest countries have become clear beneficiaries of globalization. In the creation of a worldwide working class, their role is no longer to be poor. They constitute part of the global middle class, a growing international phenomenon, which does not identify its interests with those of the poor of the earth, with the laboring poor of Bangladesh, Brazil or Indonesia, even less with the struggling self-employed of the Asian, African and South American cities, and not at all with a peasantry eking out a fragile living on the rural 'periphery', where a majority of humankind nevertheless still live.

The repercussions of these events upon both the objective and subjective position of the majority of the people in the West cannot be over-emphasized.

For one thing, there has been a major shift in perception in the relationship between rich and poor. In the early industrial period, the rich lived in a style that affronted the industrial workers. In every town and city, away from smoke borne on the prevailing wind, the mill-owners and industrialists lived in ornate mansions with ornamental ironwork and crystal conservatories, shielded from the road by large trees. Some fled the neighborhood where their fortunes had been made, and settled in even more desirable locations. The rich were always regarded ambiguously: they might have been seen as usurpers of the necessities of the poor, although this was balanced by a deference on the part of some of the poor, who hoped to gain by their loyalty and service to the rich.

Wealth creation

Poverty and injustice were always a significant political issue. While workers worked long hours for rewards that barely procured them the means of subsistence, the manufacturers indulged themselves and their families with luxury goods, foreign travel and the choicest foods unseen in the houses of the poor. One of the – perhaps unexpected – outcomes of the death of socialism and the power of globalization is that virtually everyone in the West is now united around the inclusive project of 'wealth-creation'.

If we want to understand why growing global inequality meets with only slender popular resistance, this may give a clue. It seems that *divisions between rich and poor have been submerged in a common quest for more wealth.* In other words, the majority has accepted that the only hope of a better life lies not in a fairer distribution of the wealth of the world but in the creation of much more money, which may be applied to improve their position. A universal commitment to economic growth and expansion will waft the whole population upwards into capitalism's realm of freedom. It is now the objective of international financial institutions, the World Trade Organization, governments of the G-8 and the transnationals to impose this 'settlement' upon the whole world. Unfortunately for them, the peoples of India, Bangladesh, Brazil or Mexico, receiving little benefit from this universal dedication to wealth-creation, do not always see the wisdom of this ideological structure. Indeed, the experience of people in the so-called 'developing' world is reminiscent of that endured by the workers of Britain of the early 19th century.

Of course, there are differences. People live in other climates and cultures, inheritors of other religions and ethnicities. There are varying degrees to which non-economic resources are shared, in order to humanize some of the brutalities of urbanization; an urbanization which may or may not be accompanied by industrialization. In Jakarta, Dhaka and Mexico City, for instance, manufacturing industry is widespread, much as it was in the early years of the growth of Manchester; while in Delhi and Mumbai (Bombay), there are extensive service sectors where many people make a livelihood in the shadow of commercial, governmental or bureaucratic activity, as in early 19th-century London.

In spite of all this, the inhabitants of the slums of São Paulo, Manila or Dhaka suffer want and insecurity familiar to the workers of Britain in the early industrial period. People are always poor in the same way. Hunger, insufficiency and sickness know nothing of cultural difference, but torment the body and spirit of

Hindu, animist, Nigerian or Burmese without discrimination.

And with the spread of the global market system to virtually every country on earth, the strategies for survival on which people rely show extraordinary convergence. The workers in the spinning mills and weaving sheds of Jakarta and the industrial cities of China are subject to the same evils that shaped the sensibility of the working class in Britain – wages below subsistence, long hours of labor, absence of social benefits, effective denial of the right to combine, brutal overseers.

From Rio to Mumbai

The children working in Victorian observer Henry Mayhew's London of the 1850s[5] – the mudlarks scavenging among the coal-barges in the Thames, the maids incarcerated in attics – have their counterparts in the street children earning a few opportunistic rupees in the markets of Mumbai, the children deprived of all possessions except tattered clothes who live on the river-terminal of Dhaka, the maids imprisoned behind the ornamental grilles of villas in the suburbs of Rio de Janeiro.

Everything in the world has changed and yet eerily, everything remains the same. Social and economic relationships remain constant. Only the actors are different; this is what gives the pensioners of small privilege in the West such a sense of our own improvement.

How easy it is to reconcile ourselves to the sufferings of others! How readily we accommodate the exported misery, the distant wrongs and evils which have been removed from our immediate experience! How eager we are to take credit for our good fortune, and how unwilling to reflect on the basis on which it has been built, how secure it may be and whether or not it can last! The growth of the ideology of *individualism* in the West gives to the people advantaged by globalization the impression that they are indeed responsible for their own advancement; that the improvements in their lives are a reflection of their own hard work and merit.

As seen earlier, the great majority of people in the cities of the Third World are recent country-dwellers. They bring vestiges of an archaic peasant existence, memories of subsistence and an exchange-economy not based on the values of a global market. Most are employed in the informal sector, as was the case with San Francisco or Liverpool, rather than in great concentrations of industrial labor. Most are not in sweatshops subcontracted to the transnationals, but are in small workshops, employed by local companies for the home market. Most provide some service for the rich, or they exist on the leavings of the classes above them.

But this does not mean that their relation to the global rich is different from that in which we stood towards our social superiors in the recent past. Quite the contrary. Globalization has accelerated the creation of a global working class. It is not by any means homogeneous, but fragmented, involving a high proportion of women, many children, covering a vast range of activities, sub-contracted, sub-sub-contracted, whose only unity lies in the fact that they have been called into existence by the integrating power of global capital and privilege.

The diverse peoples of the earth are increasingly pressed into the service of global wealth-creation. And the most conspicuous beneficiaries of this are precisely the former working class of the West.

1 *News from Nowhere*, William Morris, Lawrence & Wishart 1977. **2** *Pathways to Paradise*, André Gorz, Pluto Press 1985. **3** *The Leisure Society*, Jeremy Seabrook, Basil Blackwell 1988. **4** *The Theory of the Leisure Class*, Thorstein Veblen, Unwin 1970. **5** *London Labour and the London Poor*, Henry Mayhew, 1851, C Griffin & Co 1861.

5 Class and globalization

**The effects of globalization on class conscious-
ness... a look at the influence of the ideology that
came with greater affluence in the rich Western
societies... the new relationship established
between the former working class in the West and
the new working class of the South.**

THE RELATIONSHIP BETWEEN the harsh visitations
of industrialism then and now has been obscured by the
urgency of Western political discourse about 'modern-
ization', 'radical change' and the 'information
revolution'. There is scarcely any constituency in the
West to support the fight against social injustice, since we
have been spectacularly advantaged by it – slowly and
hesitantly during the colonial period, but in a highly systematic way since the apparent end of imperialism, and
at a much faster pace since the end of the Soviet Union.

According to the *Financial Times*, in 1820 the ratio
in living standards between the very richest and
poorest countries was about three to one. By 1913, this
ratio had risen to 11 to one; by 1950 it was 35 to one.
It is now more than 70 to one.

The origins of this model of global development are
not obscure. It was pioneered in the colonial era by
Britain and other imperial powers, and taken over
more recently by the US. It received new impetus from
the great compromise between capital and labor in the
Western countries at the end of the Second World War,
the social peace predicated on the premise that the
poor may become less poor if the rich become richer
and richer in perpetuity. This idea has now been
embodied in the great adventure of globalization.

The neo-liberal moment of the Thatcher-Reagan
years was no such thing: it merely represented the
entrenchment of Western dominance of the world, its
power to cancel alternatives and to institutionalize

existing patterns of power, wealth and control. According to the theory, it is only by the creation of wealth, untrammeled by government or any other interference that the poor can ever hope to be lifted out of misery.

Many comforting myths are available to gain the support of the people in the West for this view of the world. Of course the seven million child workers of Bangladesh suffer; naturally, the people living on rubbish-heaps, in crumbling tenements, in bamboo houses on stilts driven into polluted waters, in hovels of plywood, polythene and other industrial detritus, present a pitiful and regrettable sight. But after all, isn't this what our societies went through during the first period of industrialism? Our recognition of the similarities and echoes of our own forebears' experience serve, not to revolt or horrify us, but to make us see in this merely a stage of development, a necessary phase in the process of growing rich, which will eventually raise those people to the levels of living and consumption enjoyed by a majority in the West.

Yet the improvements won by Western people were achieved only by the fiercest struggle and sacrifice; and their gains were, to a considerable degree, at the expense of those whose familiar suffering we have come generally believe is no concern of ours. Moreover, the struggles of the labor movement have been obscured by globalization: a working class, divided across national boundaries, is set in competition for even the most degrading and ill-paid labor. Every time we in the rich world turn on our TV sets, we see images of the poor, noses at the windowpane of our screens. And we are invited to draw our own conclusions which, more often than not, are the conclusions of wealth and privilege.

The struggle continues

The need for continuing struggle against social injustice has not gone away. It is simply that the actors are different, unrecognizable from those who were earlier at the center of these efforts. The Western working class has indeed benefited from the growing inequality of the world. If we know how to react to the global poor, this is because we were for so long on the receiving end of the humiliations and injuries of class. The excuses multiply. They are lazy. They are different. They are black. They speak a foreign language. They worship other gods.

This wider context both explains and illuminates the social landscapes within countries. It doesn't matter how much richer the rich become, as long as our own income rises in distant (although unequal) response to it. In *The Washington Post*[1] journalist Mark Shields stated that in 1960, the average pay, after taxes, for chief executives in the largest US corporations was 12 times greater than the average factory wage. By 1974, the chief executive's wages and other emoluments had increased to about 35 times that of the company's average worker. By the mid-1990s, the differential was 135 times as much. Between 1980 and 1995, the pay of Chief Executive Officers had increased by 499 per cent; company profits had averaged 145 per cent; factory wages 70 per cent. Inflation had been 85 per cent.

According to a World Bank report in 1997, the share of global income going to the richest 20 per cent was 70.2 per cent. By 1970 it was 73.9 per cent; by 1980, 76.3 per cent and by 1989, 82.7 per cent. The share of the poorest 20 per cent had dwindled from 2.3 per cent in 1960 to 1.4 per cent by 1989.

The World Bank's Development Report for 1999 in the table overleaf gives figures for the income or consumption levels of the population in the countries of the world. The figures do not refer to the ownership of assets, but simply to income or spending. They do not, therefore, express the full extent of inequalities within those countries.

In a country like Thailand, economic growth has

Income and consumption levels (selected countries)

The World Bank's figures below show the income or consumption levels of the population in the countries of the world. The figures do not refer to the ownership of assets, but simply to income, or spending. For example, the poorest 10 per cent in Brazil have a consumption level of only 1.0 per cent, whereas the wealthiest 10 per cent consume nearly 50 per cent.

Percentage share of income or consumption

COUNTRY	Poorest 10%	Poorest 20%	Richest 20%	Richest 10%
Chile	1.4	3.4	62.0	46.9
Zimbabwe	1.8	4.0	62.3	46.9
Brazil	1.0	2.6	63.0	46.7
S Africa	1.1	2.9	64.8	45.9
Nigeria	1.6	4.4	55.7	40.8
Russian Fed.	1.7	4.4	53.7	38.7
Ethiopia	3.0	7.1	47.7	33.7
India	3.5	8.1	46.1	33.5
Thailand	2.8	6.4	48.4	32.4
US	1.8	5.2	46.4	30.5
UK	2.6	6.6	43.0	27.3
Australia	2.0	5.9	41.3	25.4
Canada	2.8	7.5	39.3	23.8
Germany	3.3	8.2	38.5	23.7

Human Development Report 2001, UNDP.

been spectacular. The International Labour Organization reports that in 1961, at the time of the country's first National Development Plan, the annual per capita income was 2,700 baht. By 1995, this had risen to 68,405 baht, a 28-fold increase. This development has had some small redistributive effect; but it has required a colossal development, in which more than 20 per cent of the country's population is concentrated around Bangkok, with all the infrastructural problems this implies, as well as the pollution, overcrowding and resource depletion. But the sheer quantity of 'development' required for a small shift in injustice suggests that if this is to be the model for reduction in poverty, the further growth and development required would be almost unlimited. If this model is transposed to India (and there is no other currently available), where the population is twenty times greater, the levels of degradation of the environment and the conditions in the cities are beyond imagination.

Enough versus more

It has become axiomatic in the Western democracies that as long as the disposable income of the majority continues to rise, social harmony will be maintained. The fact that the proportion of national (or global) income going to the poor may be falling does not alter this perception. People judge their economic well-being from the point of view of their own previous experience: if they see improvement in their own lives, they are not antagonized by the greater advantages accruing to those richer than they.

But this is not the whole story. Indeed, nothing ever is. When people make comparisons between their own life-situation and that of others, it is called 'keeping up with the Joneses'. This has become a cliché to indicate people's obsession with neighbors and peer-groups. It begs a significant question, namely, who are the Joneses trying to keep up with? Clearly, the Joneses embody an idea of permanent striving. They are an abstraction, incarnation of the notion that 'enough' is no longer definable in the global economy. In the 1960s, Clive Jenkins, an articulate trade union leader in part of the then new economy (communications), said: 'The most beautiful word in the English language is *more*'.

That statement indicated that the trade union and labor movement had definitively allied itself with the very system which had made the existence of the labor movement necessary. It symbolized the coming together of the antagonists of industry into a new partnership and the joint project of continuous growth and expansion.

This same fateful alliance has linked the destiny of

the majority of people in the rich countries with that of the global rich, and turned them into aspirants to a world-wide middle class; with the consequences for the re-structuring of the global order that we have seen.

The whole world in our hands

The rhetoric accompanying globalization has, for a long time, made any assessment of its real impact on people's lives all but impossible. The flows of trade, the growth of GNP, and all the other economic indicators are well known. All speak of prodigious expansion and development in the past 25 years. But more profound social and psychological change cannot be read in economic statistics. There are also sub-political shifts in temperament and sensibility, things that everyone feels and knows, but are rarely articulated.

It is a truism that the world has shrunk. The ethnic diversity of faces on the streets of the Western cities confirms increasing interdependence between the countries of the world. More than 150 languages are spoken in New York. Restaurants offer exotic cuisines from Ethiopia, Lebanon and Ukraine to Indonesia and Mexico, all within a few hundred yards of one another. The people of Europe are familiar with beaches in Goa, Phuket, Langkawi and Acapulco. Canadians can eat vegetables from Chile and garlic from China, while Australians jet in coffee beans from Papua New Guinea and green curry sauces from Thailand. Articles of daily wear bought in the shopping malls come from Guatemala or Bangladesh, made from fabrics woven in Taiwan, Korea or Thailand. Shoes have been made in Brazil or India, children's toys are stamped Made in China. Tourism is now the world's biggest industry: it saw 650 million arrivals in 2000, generating $455 billion (£303 billion). It seems that there are no more foreign countries.

But there are. This widening of horizons has also been accompanied by a narrowing of interest in these places, except insofar as they serve us: the air-conditioned beach-house, the quality of hotel catering, the value for money of cheap fabrics and souvenirs, the seating arrangements for the promised Mogul banquet in the hotel in Agra; would you recommend Kuwait Airlines and what is the safety record of Air Lanka? Has civil conflict in this country or the outbreak of a deadly virus in that one deterred visitors? Is it *zlotys* in Poland and *rupiah* in Bali or vice-versa? Has the banking crisis in Thailand led to a more favorable exchange-rate? Is crime a serious threat to the golden beaches of Rio? Do we really need medical insurance for Kenya?

Everything suggests an agreeable expansion in our lives and experience. But it is also true that we now read holiday brochures to discover what is really going on in the world. This is, after all, our playground, and we don't want the fun spoiled by too many stories of flood, famine, earthquake and disaster to which, it seems, our favorite spots on the globe are all too prone. Even less do we want to know about the corruption of this country, the economic downturn, the overthrow of this military ruler or that president, an ethnic cleansing here, an outbreak of cholera somewhere else. This is not of interest, and if we say so, it isn't news, since, news, like everything else, is market-driven; and we are the market and we are the drivers.

It is possible to appreciate the growing accessibility of the world while turning away from what actually goes on in it – at least in the godforsaken hinterland, the outback, the bush, the jungle, the slums, the shanties, the remote areas. We don't mind leaving the beaten track for something unspoiled, a rare species in undisturbed woodland, but we don't want poverty, filth and disease rammed down our throat, thank you very much.

If it seems unfair to cherry-pick the advantages of the Third World while largely ignoring its problems, there are precedents for this. After all, if even George

W Bush didn't know the name of the Prime Minister of India or the military ruler of Pakistan (before the 11 September 2001 crisis), why should it matter what we know? It hasn't done him much harm, and he is the leader of the free world. Why should we fill our heads with such details, when there is a life to be lived, fun to be had, a night to be danced away?

In our name

The people now being integrated into the new global order are doing so in our name, since this is enforced by international financial institutions, governments and transnational companies. And the way this is happening is – or rather, until recently, was – quite well known to us. The people in the dangerous factories and mills, children laboring as domestics or on construction sites, miners and weavers, day-laborers and porters, vendors of fruit and vegetables on the sidewalks, sellers of cigarettes, electronic games and plastic toys, scavengers among the garbage and child beggars on the railway terminals, are all doing their work in the same way and in the same conditions that we did until the day before yesterday, If we do not wish to acknowledge them, this is because we have been there and we have done that. Or rather, it has all been done to us.

We are now complicit in doing it to them. Here lies the secret of Western disengagement from a world in which our lives are more directly and profoundly implicated than ever before. We recognize ourselves as we were. It is a strange irony that in almost every town and city in Britain there have been published books of old photographs, often under the title *The Way We Were*, recalling the images of our own – now distant – past, and reminiscent of similar (largely untaken) pictures of our counterparts today in the cities of the South.

But reluctance to acknowledge our kinship with them is because we also recognize our new role in the changed division of labor. For if people are always poor in the same way, if poverty and want take the same toll of humanity, privilege also expresses itself in the same way everywhere. If we now know how to issue orders, to tell others what to do; if we use the imperious tones of those with power – however limited that small power may be – this is because we were profoundly penetrated by them, at the time when we were on the receiving end of the same orders, the same cold requests, the same cruel civility, when we waited upon the rich, filed through their factory doors, bowed and scraped before them, minded their bossy children, begged them for work and entreated their charity.

We know by instinct our new roles in the drama of globalization. We know exactly how to perform. We are word-perfect – like perpetual understudies, who get a chance to show what they can do when the star is drunk or has broken an ankle.

Of course we do not wish to acknowledge our present-day kinship with the petty tyrants, the *memsahibs*, the givers of orders and issuers of threats to those beneath them, because *we* were beneath them for so long. Why should we not exult in our new-found freedom, however limited? We know now there are others lower than we are in the global order, and we shall make them feel the sting of their subordination.

If there was one law for the rich and another for the poor, we have now passed under the jurisdiction of the former.

Force of circumstance

There is nothing *personal* in all this. It is all a question of circumstances; and though we struggled to improve our own position, we had no part in the degradation of today's poor. We will be nice to the waiter in the hotel in Gambia, and we will take something to the poor family in Isaan whose daughter we met in the bar. We joke with the children selling flowers on the street, and take photographs of the artful beggars and pretty wheedlers in the bazaar, so reminiscent of the urchins in Dickens.

But now it is our turn, the new arrivals in the position of the eternal and growing global middle-class; with the glorious and triumphal difference – unknown to our fearful, uptight predecessors – that those beneath us do not present the slightest threat or challenge. They are not organized. They are powerless. They are there to wait on us. They exist for our comfort and amusement. Happy dispensation of Providence that has seen fit to grant us our just desserts after centuries of thankless labor, and has placed a whole world at our beck and call.

How we got here

How this came about has not been without its problems. The process has been the object of much discussion, speculation and academic research. During the 1950s and 60s, there was debate in Europe on the theory of *embourgeoisement* of the working class.

Resist!

There are many movements of resistance to an order that integrates class hierarchies within a single globalizing economy. The Brazilian Landless Workers' Movement is one of the most successful grass-roots movements in the world. In a country where less than 3 per cent of the population owns two-thirds of Brazil's arable land, 25 million people struggle to survive as landless laborers. In 1985, hundreds of people took over an unused plantation and established a co-opera-tive. In 1987 they gained title to the land. The Landless Workers' Movement was born (*Movimento dos Trabalhadores Rurais Sem Terra*, MST). Today more than 250,000 families have gained land titles to over 15 million acres. In 1999, 25,099 families occupied land; and in 2001, there were more than 70,000 families awaiting government recognition of land rights. There has been resistance from landown-ers. More than 1000 people have been killed in the past 10 years over land conflicts. The Movement embodies the germ of an alternative way of living: by the establishment of food security and self-reliance, by the creation of food co-operatives and small agricultural indus-tries. There is an extensive literacy program and there are more than 1,000 primary schools in MST settlements. ■

It arose out of the rising prosperity of the 1950s (itself constructed on the security provided by the welfare state in the post-war period), and the coming of the consumer society. The question then was, have the rising income, access to certain consumer goods – TV, washing-machine, refrigerator, as well as holidays abroad and greater domestic comfort – fundamentally altered the sensibility of the working class and made it more like that of the middle class?

Much of this discussion was prompted by the decline in support for socialist and labor parties in Europe. Sociologist Ferdynand Zweig[2] accepts the inherent conflict between capital and labor, but he claims that the welfare state has cushioned the workers against the worst rigors of insecurity and unemployment, so that they have been turned into 'full and willing partners in the acquisitive society'. Zweig talks of the 'conversion' of the antagonists of capitalism to its own creed.

Much of this debate now appears arcane and slightly absurd, given the effects of globalization, but it is clear that the shifts detected very soon after the Second World War, the period of the greatest 'success' of collectivist government intervention, in setting up the welfare state, already marked a subterranean – 'sub-political' in EP Thompson's terms – change in the temper of the people; a change that has become more apparent with time.

It is a fundamental shift, which parallels the great transformation that took place in the movement from agrarian to industrial economy. It was an error to assume that once industrial society was established, the same people would more or less continue to occupy the same position in perpetuity. This was partly a result of the ideological certainties of Marx, the hardening of these into a totalizing belief-system, dogmatic adherence to them by his followers, and their realization within a Soviet Union that invested the ideology with the sanctity of secular scripture. The toll which this took upon actually existing humanity, particularly those who dissented from its revelations (or the interpretation of these as decreed by the ruling class in the Soviet Union) – is a matter of record.

What Marx said

Something of these same certainties pervaded political and academic circles in the West, where generations of Leftists found meaning, faith and sometimes lucrative careers in textual analyses of what Marx said or meant or might have meant. The shadow of Marx haunted discussions of the working class everywhere. And what was a temporary phenomenon – the industrial worker of the mid- to late-19th and early 20th centuries – came to be seen as a definitive incarnation of class. This has proved a conservative and disabling fixation. Although, as the sociologist Richard Scase argues, class relationships within capitalism remain unchanged, nevertheless, in people's subjective apprehension, 'at best, class is a vague residual feature of social life'.

People see their own lives in terms of individual biography and personal details; if they succeed, they ascribe that success to personal worth or merit; if they fail, they see it as a personal deficiency. The structures of exclusion and disadvantage have become largely invisible to those afflicted by them. Scase insists, with Marx, that no matter how people see their social position, 'relations of exploitation and control' persist, 'irrespective of the perceptions and assumptions of participating actors'.

In recent decades we have witnessed again the adaptability and resourcefulness of capital. Technological advances, especially in communications, have permitted capital to move with extraordinary speed across the globe – it is a truism that one trillion dollars are on the move each day.

Transnational corporations are now more powerful than many national governments: of the richest one hundred economic entities in the world, 50 are corporations and 50 are countries. In such a context, how will anything remain static? Yet, surprisingly, this is what happened to the benumbed political resistance to capitalism, with its unimaginative versions of a Utopia, dreary and pedestrian compared with the shifting castles of dreams created by the culture of capitalism. Why imagine that humanity – so readily reshaped by the necessities of mass manufacture in the early industrial period – would remain impervious to the altered circumstances of a globalism which sweeps everything before it?

A crucial influence upon the lives of the people has been the ideological power of capitalism, especially its capacity to produce. Capitalism has for 200 years held out a promise, not only of an end to poverty, but also of riches beyond compare. Yet poverty is far from ended, even though riches beyond compare have indeed been created. Out of this very abundance, strange new poverties have been conjured. A profound subjective sense of insufficiency has arisen; and not only among the poor and marginalized. Everyone feels poor, confronted by the limitlessness of what the global system offers. A common complaint of the well-to-do from North America to Australasia is 'we can't afford it'; although their lives are already distinguished by luxuries unknown in earlier times to even rulers and princes. When the meaning of 'enough' is lost, even the richest no longer know the meaning of satisfaction.

Human need and economic necessity

Economists who, when the science was in its infancy produced good reasons why it was the fate of the majority to remain in a state of chronic insecurity and want, now exuberantly express a quite different ideology. The message of globalization is quite the opposite of the gloomy story of the past, which earned economics the name of 'the dismal science'.

Class and globalization

In his book, *Pursuing Happiness*, US economist Stanley Lebergott[3] makes a brave attempt to equate human need with economic necessity. He is at pains to assimilate the most extravagant and frivolous objects of consumption with the supreme governing principle of human life which is the search for greater happiness, and therefore as vital as the most obvious item needful for survival. He writes: 'Attempts to distinguish "essential" desires from "false" ones have been unending and futile.'

He continues: 'In the 18th century, economist Sir James Steuart contrasted "physical" necessities with "political" ones. "Physical necessities" were pretty much those consumed by Robinson Crusoe. "Political necessities" were those added by custom and civilization. But even brute "subsistence" was defined to include much more than bread and water. Even Malthus, the 19th-century population doomsayer, included "political necessities" in his list of coarse 'means of subsistence'. The "iron law of wages" of 19th-century German socialist Lasalle was no less inclusive. Marx, too, included much more than "material wants such as food, clothing etc". He included "so-called necessary wants" which inevitably "depended on the habits and degree of comfort" in which workers were raised... The drama still rings out from such fearsome words as "subsistence" and "immiseration". But the minimum consumption level for Marx and Lasalle, as well as Steuart and Adam Smith, was never defined by life on an ice floe. For them, all the "means of subsistence" escalated with historical and social change.'

This version of the world omits to state that it is not simply that 'culture' and 'civilization' have moved on; but that the expansion of markets has actually become the main preoccupation of culture and civilization. When human purposes have been captured and controlled by institutions that are supposed to serve human beings, some very strange phenomena must be expected. The argument that needs change in sympathetic accord with alterations in cultures is one thing; but when the adding of value to human need, the intensification of marketing, the penetration of our lives by a buy-in culture becomes the be-all and end-all of social endeavor, we have long passed the point at which our needs merely reflect society. The market has long ago colonized society, and is now seeking to conquer life itself, by genetic control and manipulation of crops, animals and human beings, not for the sake of some greater good of humanity, but in order to make profits in the ever-expanding universe of the market economy.

There was fierce resistance to the designation of people as mere 'hands', appendages of industrial machinery engaged and discarded according to market need. But to their role as servants of the market in a more polished and acceptable guise of consumers, there have been fewer objections, except – as Lebergott points out – by self-appointed moralists and intellectuals.

If we want to know what happened to the working class, we should look not only at those who labor now in the Third World in the way we did, but also at the influences which have transformed the significance of who we are and what we do. André Gorz pointed out that work was what people did; now a job is something you have[4] – a change in our time no less epochal than that which convulsed the early 19th century.

1 *The Washington Post*, 22 August 1995. **2** *The Worker in an Affluent Society*, Ferdynand Zweig, Heinemann 1961. **3** *Pursuing Happiness*, Stanley Lebergott, Princeton University Press 1993. **4** *Farewell to the Working Class*, André Gorz, Pluto Press 1982.

6 Goodbye to the working class?

Examining the apparent disappearance of the working class... and the re-emergence of class in the shape of a middle class... and an underclass... How globalization has created this illusion.

ANDRÉ GORZ DESCRIBES a world in which human need can readily be answered, but where alienated production must be kept going in order to feed alienated consumption. 'What do we need?' he asked. 'What do we desire? What do we lack in order to fulfill ourselves, to communicate with others, to lead more relaxed lives and establish more loving relations? Economic forecasting and political economy have nothing to offer here... Deliberately and systematically, they provide us with new wants and new scarcities, new types of luxury and new senses of poverty, in conformity with capitalism's need for profitability and growth. Capital has at its service a number of strategists who are capable of manipulating our most intimate desires in order to impose their products upon us by means of the symbols with which they are charged.'[1]

Gorz says technological change has broken the power of industrial workers, whose role in radical change has now been replaced by those struggling for autonomy *outside* a productive process, which is decreasingly articulated to human need, but pursues its own internal necessities. He saw the women's movement and the Greens as having replaced the workers as the central actors in transformation.

His assertion that the working class is no longer central to radical change is reflected more widely, in the sense that it has virtually disappeared from political and social discourse, both in the United States, and to a lesser extent, in Europe.

In discussions of class in the US, much is heard of 'middle-class families' or 'middle-income groups'. The words 'working class' never had the same resonance in the US as in Europe, because, as sociologist Peter Drucker points out, workers (in the sense of people 'who make or move things' in his rather eccentric classification) never constituted more than 40 per cent of the US population even in the 1950s.

The working class was written out of American society early on. Not for the first time, this has served as a model for the rest of the 'developed' world. There, too, silence has fallen upon the extinguished role of the working class, not only in its Marxist sense as a redemptive global force, but even as historical reality. This has appeared especially in the way former socialist, laborist or workers' political parties abandoned those in whose name they were formed. The creation of 'New Labour' in Britain was a signal that the party had cut itself free of its roots, although it sometimes coyly refers to them as its 'natural supporters'.

The funerary orations over the end of the working class, however, cannot conceal the new landscape, in which an ugly new factor has been discovered; namely an 'underclass'. This brutal word refers to a minority of people in the rich world, something between one-quarter and one-third of the population, who live in poverty.

Losers and 'no-hopers': the underclass

The idea of an underclass first appeared in a book by US writer Ken Auletta[2] in 1982. These are people who do not participate in the mainstream activities of the society that shelters them. It is not precisely synonymous with poverty, but is associated with a chaotic social life; with criminality, dropping out of education and work, a breakdown in stable relationships. The presence of an 'underclass' in societies that deny the existence of class is an anomaly few care to address.

This 'underclass' didn't come from nowhere. Its discovery in the years of the Reagan presidency occurred when it had become clear that governmental attempts to alleviate poverty had been unsuccessful. The naming of an underclass exonerated government from any responsibility for their fate. It confirms and strengthens a version of society in which the morally and socially outcast would not help themselves and therefore must take their chances in the world. This re-moralization of the capitalist system, where a majority participate in work and consumption in exemplary ways, dispenses with minorities who do not. These are electoral nonentities with no purchasing power, the 'losers' in a society in which most see themselves as winners, or potential winners. The no-hopers can be left to their own devices – a policy which had its effect, as cargoes of injured humanity were brought out of the ghettoes and public housing schemes of the US to perish or to survive in ill-appointed public hospitals and institutions – dumping grounds for the waste management of an increasingly industrialized humanity.

Of course, the underclass has its antecedents in the history of industrial life. They are the re-incarnation of a distinction well known to Victorian England, between the 'respectable' and the 'rough', the 'deserving' and the 'undeserving' poor; to which problem the Poor Law Amendment Act of 1834 had addressed itself with all the punitive fury of those who have against those who have nothing. Social researchers, observers and reformers of the 19th century from Henry Mayhew to Charles Booth chronicled the fate of the beggars, orphans, prostitutes, scavengers, confidence tricksters and unfortunates of the city streets. These were also the people dismissed by Marx as 'Lumpenproletariat', which meant the habitually criminal, the stupid and the unbelonging of the working class.

Indeed, the distinction between the deserving and

undeserving was never completely lost in Europe. The resentment of the prosperous against post-war welfarism focused on those who got everything although they contributed nothing. Single mothers, the workshy, migrants, alcoholics and the mentally ill have all, at one time or another, been objects of popular anger; to which categories of 'asylum-seekers', 'drug addicts', 'perverts' and 'pedophiles' have been added.

For much of the 20th century, the undeserving or 'underclass', were contained within working-class communities. Each neighborhood around factories and workshops had its deficient, its failures, its weak and incompetent. Sometimes, these were made to feel their position, but usually they were held by the harsh disciplines of community. Rough justice was meted out to wrongdoers; those able but unwilling to work were made to feel their neighbors' disapproval. But there are numerous stories of motherless children taken in by neighbors and brought up as their own.

It wasn't all charitable – wedlock meant more of the lock than of the wedding and women who became pregnant before marriage were severely treated (as were their children). But there is no doubt that a communitarian sentiment protected many of those subsequently relegated to the underclass, partly because the coercive agents of the state – those administering grudging welfare payments – did their work all too effectively, and people were unwilling to offer up defaulters to the mercies of government functionaries.

Post-war wealth

However, in the post-Second World War era most people became wealthier. They moved out of the old communities, which were obliterated to make way for new estates, tower blocks and all the amenities now at the disposal of the contemporary underclass. People retreated to the suburbs and new estates, they ceased renting and bought their homes. This left the old, unreconstructed poor exposed and stranded. Add to this people from the old colonial empires, or in Germany, from Turkey, encouraged as economic migrants to answer (sometimes short-lived) labor shortages, and the composition of the old city center streets was transformed.

Migrants were usually from small communities, peasant societies, the same origin of a working class formed so long ago. But urban life had by this time virtually effaced all such memories of the indigenous communities. They regarded migrants with the double estrangement that came, not only from unfamiliarity with those of other ethnicities and religions, but also from the appearance of recent peasants in the long-established urban environment of European cities. Racism, xenophobia and unemployment alienated many of the next generation of these migrants; to which drugs, crime and exclusion from the consumer paradise did their bit to identify the new 'underclass'.

Nazi connotations

The word underclass has echoes of the Nazi term *Untermensch* – sub-humans – a dehumanizing word used to describe the Jews, homosexuals and mentally-ill people that the Nazis drove into the death camps. Underclass echoes the racist response to the poor of the contemporary world, for non-whites do make up a disproportionate number of those labeled in this way. The concept of underclass indicates, not merely a minority in the West, but also suggests a majority in the Third World; and the history of racist ideology in the great imperial adventure of the Western world is well known.

When the 'underclass' first appeared (not under that name) in the early years of prosperity in the 1950s and 60s, they were seen as a remnant, left behind by general improvements. It was assumed that prosperity would soon enclose everyone in an inclusive embrace. To those who showed reluctance to be benefited in this way, social workers were assigned to do 'casework' intended to reconcile such people with those whose lives had been conspicuously bettered. When it became clear that there were structural reasons for the persistence of such misfits, this was sometimes ascribed to the survival of 'medieval families', a minority whose values and mores preceded industrial society and who would continue to present – minor but intractable – problems for the foreseeable future.

To be a member of the underclass is the contemporary equivalent of belonging to the 'lower orders' as they were described in pre-industrial society. The difference is that this version of the lower orders constitutes a minority, whereas at an earlier period they were in the majority. As such, they show little resistance to being labeled as a caste apart. Since the vote is the only social weapon they have (apart from crime) this is unlikely to be effective against privilege.

The underclass has a useful function in a society where most conceive of themselves as middle class. They serve as a warning to keep the rest of us in line. Here is a strange paradox. The people whose incontinent and often brutalized lives are so disordered, living in ghettoes or housing developments smelling of violence, piss and despair, are actually agents of social control. They impose a salutary discipline on the majority, a powerful encouragement to keep us to beaten pathways, lest our fate come to resemble theirs. They teach the wisdom of conformism and orthodoxy, the folly of dissent and the consequences of trying to live in any other manner.

Their absence of purchasing power is worse than nudity; for without it they are flayed alive each day, like souls in the poet Dante's hell. The rich can now rejoice over the decay of class conflict. Enjoyment of their wealth is no longer contested by people animated by 'the politics of envy'. We are all now content to pin our hopes onto existing patterns of wealth-creation, disinclined to ponder the new forms of impoverishment and insufficiency engendered by the creation of unlimited wealth.

New poverty, new classes in the global economy

There is a distinction between the underclass and the poor. For with the integration of the global economy, new kinds of poverty, and new classes of people *who feel that they are poor* have come into existence.

Globalization now reaches into every aspect of the lives of the people. Discussions about poor people, however, have made little concession to this, and have remained focused on national poverty. But the character and consciousness of the poor have also been reshaped by the processes which determine the sensibility of the rich. This makes it difficult to devise local (that is, national) remedies for evils that have their origins beyond national boundaries. Within the richest countries of the G-8, the gap between rich and poor continues to widen. Compensatory state benefits cannot keep pace with the distribution of rewards in the global market.

Poverty itself is constantly refined and redefined in response to global plenty. If a TV is now a basic necessity in the rich world, this is because TV has become the major medium of instruction and entertainment, the principal informant of the people about their own lives. It transmits a constant imagery of all the things we don't have and at the same time presents pictures of the poorest people in the world, the victims of floods or earthquake, displaced by civil strife or ethnic cleansing, evicted from farms or fields, or destroyed by fires raging through squatter communities. The real function of TV is ideological: its double lesson teaches us how lucky we are, but it also displays how much more we might enjoy.

In this context, to add up the cost of basic necessities and measure shortfall in income as poverty no longer suffices. Nor is it adequate to state simply

Life, health and the HDI

Every year the UN calculates a 'Human Development Index' (HDI) for all the countries of the world. It is a composite index measuring average achievement in three basic areas of human development: a long and healthy life, knowledge and a decent standard of living. Unsurprisingly, rich countries such as Norway, Australia and Canada top the list. The highest-ranked less developed country is South Korea, above Portugal. The 10 lowest-ranked countries also come as no surprise; war is just one of the factors for some of their poverty.

Highest HDI rank	Lowest HDI rank
1 Norway	**153** Mali
2 Australia	**154** Central African Republic
3 Canada	**155** Chad
...	**156** Guinea-Bissau
6 United States	**157** Mozambique
...	**158** Ethiopia
14 United Kingdom	**159** Burkina Faso
...	**160** Burundi
19 Aotearoa/New Zealand	**161** Niger
...	**162** Sierra Leone
27 South Korea	
...	
34 Argentina	

Human Development Report 2001, UNDP.

that 'poverty has become relative', as though that alone could account for the *violence* of poverty in the richest societies the world has ever known.

The usual response now is to emphasize the creation of wealth, since it is assumed that this will eventually (when?) lift the poor out of their condition, despite the lack of evidence that this alleviates inequality. Governments now consider tax-breaks for the rich a greater generator of well-being for the poor than any effort to divert for their benefit some of the proceeds of the making of fortunes.

It is now considered improper even to discuss redistribution. The official reason for this is a very ancient one, namely that it interferes with the dynamic of wealth-creation.

But there is a more compelling reason for the

silence over distributive justice. The rich are no longer constrained to pay taxes that might be deployed for the relief of poverty. Those who in the 19th century resisted extending the franchise to poor people were terrified that these would vote to dispossess the wealthy peaceably, through the ballot-box. This possibility has now been canceled. The opportunities open to the rich to avoid tax, by means of off-shore havens, secret accounts and chains of electronic concealment, ensure that even if a majority voted to limit their wealth, they could avoid the consequences.

Money walks

The new mobility of wealth has endowed it with magical properties. Nothing must now impede the work of high endeavor that is the making of money. The rich are now no longer monopolists of the necessities of the poor, but the creators of wealth, without whom the poor will be even poorer. In other words, the poor now appear as dependents, rather than victims, of the rich. The poor no longer envy them their good fortune; indeed, they identify their own fate with theirs, hoping that some of it will flow in their direction. Social peace is attained at last.

But poverty itself has changed under the globalizing imperative, and does not present to the world the aspect with which we have long been familiar.

Most ruling élites, if they think about poverty at all, have an antiquated view of it. It still evokes archaic images – ragged starvelings, sickly children, unbalanced diets, the squalid housing, unemployment, ignorance and fatalism. The iconography of early industrialism is the ghost in the high-tech machine. Memories of that time have an eerie afterlife, which still inhabits politics and attitudes in an environment where everything is altered, yet nothing is changed.

Poverty has metamorphosed under the impact of globalization. While there is still a residuum of an earlier version, poverty now means something else. *The poor are no longer inhabitants of this or that country; they are the excluded of the global market.* This is bound to influence the temper and psyche of the poor.

Poverty – like wealth – could not remain untouched by the compulsions of globalism. The poor of a new generation are no longer created by the workings of a national economy; they are the orphaned progeny of a global market; and they behave accordingly. Much that seems incomprehensible flows from this change, at once momentous and invisible.

Politicians who refer to 'social exclusion' are avoiding a more intractable reality. Since the majority of social activities now take place within spaces created by the market, they are really referring to market exclusion. When the French Prime Minister Lionel Jospin said 'Yes to the market economy, No to market society', he was already too late. The market has already colonized society. It is now staking its claim to control over existence itself, the whole of Creation – the bio-industries, genetic modification, the possibility of breeding bothersome genes out of tainted people, the re-design of human beings, nourishing them with industrially-generated foods, growing spare parts for bodies on other animals, preparing a storehouse of body-tissue in laboratory cultures. Why should the global market pause at the portals of society, when it has already invaded the innermost sanctuaries of life itself?

Gone shopping

In Britain in 1999, the largest item of household expenditure was, for the first time in history, devoted to leisure activities; overtaking the proportion spent on any other goods or services, including food, health and housing. Shopping is now the largest leisure pursuit. Non-participants in these central social activities are seriously disadvantaged.

That they are evictees of a global market, and not of

national life, is the reason why many of the young linger around malls and gallerias, the great enclosures of merchandise where all the significant cultural exchanges occur. This is true of the rich countries, North America, Europe, Aotearoa/New Zealand and Australia, and equally of Thailand, Brazil, Indonesia and Mexico. 'Pioneered', as it were, in the US, evidence of the violence engendered by this form of exclusion was formerly met by complacent Europeans with 'Oh, that's America, what can you expect?', and 'It couldn't happen here'. Such responses are no longer heard.

We now know that whatever baleful social phenomenon occurs in the US, it will unfailingly make its appearance around the world. These variants on poverty migrate at double-quick speed, whether drugs of first choice, multiple addictions, access by schoolchildren to handguns, the sexualizing of small children – these are some of the violent poverties shaped by the exigencies of the market: the low-esteem, high-price, added-value impoverishment of new generations, born to poverties undreamed-of by an antique working class shaped by other squalors in the slums of Victorian Britain.

A new culture of poverty is now visible all over the 'developed' world. And it is identical. Older versions of poverty have not been entirely displaced; the poor-but-honest, frugality, stoicism and pride. These still exist, but have been eclipsed by the changing sensibility of the age. *The poor have been re-shaped in the image of the rich.* They have been subject to the same relentless advertising, the same exhortations to get, to have and to spend. *Their* appetites have also been kindled, *their* desire for the things of the world aroused; they have been exposed to the breakdown of self-restraint, the need for market-driven belonging. But from the poor, the money required to participate has been withheld.

Blow your mind

The alien culture of 'advanced poverty', modernized want, characterizes the whole industrial world. It displays the same features in all countries: nihilistic, amoral, exulting in the expression of its aggressive purposelessness. It generates rising crime, drug-use, violence, addictions, racism, peer-driven competitiveness and gang warfare. Its victims are exiles of the market, a tenantless community of exclusion: the teenage runaways, the elective homeless, the non-voters, the dead souls of democracy, the dropped out and uncounted, those surviving or perishing on the margin, the mercenaries of transnationals, at war with each other over logos and brand-names.

Drugs are the supreme commodity uniting the globalization of poor lives articulated to an elusive elsewhere. Drugs are the lubricant which eased the nationally excluded into a limbo of supranational segregation.

The spread of drug culture is associated in the West with the time when the global economy was first opened up, when mind-altering substances from Burma, Afghanistan, Pakistan, Colombia and other exotic locations became commonplace on the streets of the West's cities. At this time, from the 1960s to the 1980s, military dictatorships all over South and Central America, Asia and Africa, were making the world safe for globalization, by the most savage oppression of their own people – Marcos in the Philippines; Zia-ul-Haq in Pakistan; the Brazilian, Uruguayan and Argentine generals; Paraguay's Stroessner; Indonesia's Suharto; Bokassa in the Central African Republic; Mobutu in Zaire/DR Congo; South Africa's apartheid regime; Chile's Pinochet and Ershad in Bangladesh. Under the pretext of 'containment of communism' (already in an advanced state of decay), the economies under the tutelage of 'strong men' made great strides towards economic integration. British Prime Minister

Goodbye to the working class

Margaret Thatcher, in her praise of General Pinochet, pointed out that the Chilean economy was 'transformed' under his abrasive rule. Indeed it was; and to prove it, grapes, apples and vegetables from that liberated land could be bought wherever there was money to pay for them.

Drugs arrived in the West by the same market mechanisms which facilitated the export of basic foodstuffs from hungry countries. It is interesting to note that whenever drugs are reported recovered by the police, it is their *street-value* rather than their *market-value* that is stressed; this protects the sanctity of the market. The question is not so much the presence of traffickers, dealers and profiteers in mind-altering substances (by that token, the directors of virtually all Western media conglomerates would be arraigned as criminals), as what absences, what aching emptiness and what voids, created the spectacular *demand* for products that enabled people to transcend their own good fortune, to escape from societies based upon escapism, to rise above a life already elevated far above anything seen in the history of humanity?

As the industrial base melted away, goods made on our doorstep ceased to be the home-made, familiar objects of everyday life. Even the most matter-of-fact necessities were wafted in from elsewhere. The simplest things – shirts and coats, shoes and toys – were supplied from distant lands, as were electronic goods, refrigerators, TVs, labor-saving appliances. Once producers had been banished from sight, the space between producers and consumers was filled with hymns composed by advertisers and commissioned by their manufacturers. The plainest objects – a jacket, a sports shoe – became haloed with mystery and desirability. They took up their place in the palaces of merchandise, the shopping malls which appeared in the center of every community in the Western world.

The violence of market exclusion is seen in the

obsession of the young with brand names, logos and all the emblems that signify belonging. Here is another pleasing convergence: when the young excluded bear on their person the publicity of transnational companies, not only have the poor ceased to be enemies of the rich, but they obligingly promote the rich's interests.

They are united in new forms of subjection, bonded to the cargo cults of the transnationals. Their psyche has been formed by technologies from the same elsewhere that has no locator, the placeless sites where things are made. The instruments that transmit the music and images, the sounds and sights of the world are not created within view. They come into their lives from the dark places of the world, cleansed of blood and sweat; shining objects ritually purified by publicity and the remoteness between producers and consumers – a no-one's-land of concealment and forgetting.

Wasted humanity

'Relative' poverty in the rich societies has been misunderstood. It has been taken to mean relative to what others have. It is actually relative to the limitless capacity of the global industrial engines to produce. And relative to that, everyone is poor. What money can buy offers perpetual instruction in our own inadequacies. And this leads to an even more closely guarded secret; namely, the *possibility* that even inclusion within the market may also be pathology, since it confronts everyone with the bleak prospect of insufficiency in a world in which wants have become infinite. Poverty has become the natural state of all humanity, even of the seven million millionaires of the world; and the imagination has been colonized by visions of perpetual increase.

This is part of a dynamic process. As material wealth accumulates, more and more human resources fall into disuse. Buying in all that is necessary is essentially a passive and uncreative form of human activity – no matter what ingenuity may go into the making of the money that procures these 'necessities'.

The rich see no inconvenience in this but for the poor, who are subject to the same pressures, it is felt as violence: for them, access is barred to the storehouse of global treasures, without which there is no good or full life. Demoralization hangs over poor communities, palpable as the industrial smogs that scar their landscapes: the neglected and cheerless interiors, blinds drawn till midday, escape into long hours of sleep, smudgy videos in smoky rooms, the sour breath of yesterday's drink, junk food and the junk culture – the wreckage of human resources are the invisible counterpart of the wreckage of material resources with which the earth is now littered. There is no underclass; only a poor, perishing and wasted humanity.

Class and a better life

Privilege controls all the images of the better life, which passed into private ownership long ago. Few of the poor, the 'underclass', now embody the faintest impulse towards another way of living, but seek merely, from their dependent place, to imitate those set above them. In the early 19th century, it was possible to paint images of the better world which the toilers for social justice thought they could create. William Morris, in *News From Nowhere*, evoked a world in which humanity had been released from needless toil in favor of necessary work. It is an idyllic, pre-industrial vision. All Utopian alternatives prefigure a world of abundance and ease, of which capitalist consumerism is both approximation and caricature.

From Robert Owen, early in the 19th century, with his view that human beings are molded by their cultural and physical environment, it was never difficult for reformers, socialists and visionaries to offer material versions of an alternative – often drawing on rustic pre-industrial imagery, sometimes calling upon a seemingly inexhaustible reservoir of human nostalgia. The visionary framers of a more hopeful future always described physical scenes far removed from the oppressive spectacle of daily life – whether it was the peasant or rural person eating wholesome bread and drinking ale beneath the village tree, or an idealized version of an industrial worker going about his labor in a dignified environment of orderly streets, neat artisans' houses and well-regulated factories – the images of a better world had not yet been expropriated by capitalism and sold back to the people.

Robert Owen's work at the industrial settlement of New Lanark led to a formulation of his ideas in *A New View of Society* (1813). In introducing improvements in working and living conditions for the workforce in his spinning works, he wrote: 'What are the best arrangements under which these men and their families can be well and economically lodged, fed, clothed, trained, educated, employed and governed?' This use of the passive voice was reflected in later attempts at social progress: the people have never been active participants in these reforms.

How easily the homely images of a decent life have been overwhelmed by the florid images of glamour, romance, mobility and success of the global dream factory! The very modesty of the demands of the working class and its prophets and visionaries has been swept aside by the baroque excesses of the promises of consumer capitalism. The frugal hopes of betterment were submerged in a global iconography of affluence; a sort of mass privilege from which only the poor of the earth (the majority of humanity) are banished.

1 *Farewell to the Working* Class, André Gorz, Pluto Press 1982. **2** *The Underclass*, Ken Auletta, Random House 1982.

7 The enduring injuries of class

How class has not gone away, even though it may have disappeared from both official rhetoric and consciousness of the people... how its long-term effects and injuries continue in other forms.

IN THE RICH world, many of the poor are continuing victims of the long-term effects of industrialization, processes initiated long ago, which work themselves out only slowly, often in subterranean ways, through the generations. The large proportion of the children, or even distant descendants, of migrants or former slaves among the poor is equally a long-term consequence of imperialism and its attendant racism. The ruling élites, who formerly embraced doctrines of the inferiority of the races they ruled in their colonial empires, abandoned the ideology of racism as inconvenient and distasteful in the wake of its florid expression in Europe the 1930s and 40s. But it seeped through the social strata and collected at the bottom in the substratum of exclusion, where it continues its poisonous course into the present.

One of the criticisms of class was that those born to labor had no opportunity to enter more elevated employment. Unfairness was built into the structures of society. Now that these disadvantaged classes are no longer so easily identified, there has been universal celebration over equal chances for all. The class system has been declared dead, superseded by the benefits of a new meritocratic order, in which people's social position reflects, not an inherited social position, but their true worth.

The violence of the 'meritocracy'
The belief that a meritocracy has replaced older disabilities of class is very powerful; for it represents a *collective* and *socially-created* belief that *individuals* have got where they are because of their own intrinsic

worth. It is actually to deny the great transformation experienced in the rich industrial societies, whereby many of the labor-intensive activities formerly carried out by a working class have been transferred to distant places of the world; those more effectively accomplished by machines have been transferred to capital-intensive mechanization.

The spaces created by this shift have left scope for a whole new distribution of labor within the Western industrial countries, especially those concerned with banking, financial services, insurance, tourism, catering, entertainment, health and welfare, education. Within this highly diversified employment-structure, people have been repeatedly told that where they wind up is a direct reflection of their own hard work, effort and talents.

There has been an explosion of economic activity, which has permitted many who formerly would have been destined for mine, factory or steelworks to express themselves (and sometimes to make large fortunes by doing so) in the music *industry*, the entertainment *industry*, the fashion *industry*, the film *industry*, the advertising *industry*. Those who wrote of a 'post-industrial society' were clearly premature. Far from industrial society having changed, it seems that many social activities have been industrialized and re-shaped in the image of an industrialism, which only in the more primitive form of mass manufacturing, has indeed disappeared.

The idea of meritocracy again advantages the already privileged. The myth that the social system is open to all talented people, no matter what their origin, suits the competent and the clever. It releases able people who had undoubtedly been held back by a class system which curtailed their education, used up their energies and powers, diminished their lives. It is only natural that the beneficiaries of such processes should accept the heroic role offered them by society: 'See what I have done by my own efforts.' They collude with the vanishing trick of society, whereby proud individuals stand, raised up by the sweat of their brow; which conveniently elides the oceans sweated by those in the past – and elsewhere in the present – for little or no reward.

So much for success under the system of meritocracy, equality of opportunity or whatever ideology of personal self-betterment is available. But what of failure? In a class-dominated society, those oppressed by exploitation have external factors to account for their lowly social position.

There are clearly structural economic factors in their disadvantage. This relieves individuals of having to take responsibility for elements in their life imposed from outside, and they can also console themselves that in other circumstances, they might have made something of their lives, been more successful, owned their own home, become a teacher or a doctor. But when they are told repeatedly that all have equal opportunities, in a society which insists that people are rewarded according to their merit, what conclusion should they draw? That their poverty is a result of their own social inutility? That they have their just desserts? That they are excluded because they are not considered worthy of 'inclusion'? That they are ill-rewarded, not by chance, but by some intrinsic fault in their make-up, some flaw in their character?

Criminal classes and affluent societies

The brutality of this message has fateful consequences. The poor revolt instinctively against this account of their poverty and failure. The capable, young, energetic people who find their intelligence unrecognized, and their capacities wasted, turn, naturally enough, to the only form of redress open to 'worthless' individuals – crime.

The phenomenon of rising crime in the richest societies the world has ever known is one of the great conundrums of the late 20th century. It reflects continuing social injustice within societies whose wealth has been prodigious, and in which certain individuals have been conspicuously rewarded. Those from whom these advantages are withheld fail to perceive why they are treated in this way, and they have recourse to the only remedy open to them in a society where social hope has been canceled; and that is with private answers to the injustice which imprisons them in prison-like suburbs, public housing schemes, *bidonvilles*, *favelas*, *barrios*, slums and peripheral dumping-grounds which characterize the cities of the world.

Crime is a response to an *ideology* of merit and demerit, of success and failure. It requires no great insight for the marginalized to discern that those who are so extravagantly rewarded in this society – the boy next door who becomes a football star, the girl who won the talent competition on TV, the new band created by a publicity machine, the star of this show or that TV soap, a tycoon who turns around a company one day only to be disgraced when the profits fall in the next financial year, the patent-holder of some exciting new product to hit the market – are very little different from themselves.

They understand that luck is the biggest factor in the making of fortunes, an impression fortified by the social promise implicit in the games of chance, the winning ticket, the lucky number or the sudden windfall. Distribution of wealth is random. People would scarcely be human if they meekly sank under the myth of their own absent merit or lack of the mysterious attributes which produce such destructive inequalities. It is the meager endowments of celebrity and fame, not their own inferiority which create instinctive rebellion. With no possibility of social improvement, they take the law into their own hands.

Crime is, therefore, a highly ideological phenomenon, directly related, not exactly to 'poverty' in a traditional sense, but to the structures of inequality within societies distinguished by their immense wealth. It rises in relation to growing inequality. Crime is the price worth paying by the rich for the writing out of distributive justice from the programs of all mainstream political parties in the West. The 'problem' of its containment only conceals the even more intractable problem of an injustice for which no effective remedies are now offered by anyone.

The myth of merit has displaced older interpretations of class. But the shadow of the old class structure continues to recruit large numbers of the choiceless poor into the category of the unmeritorious. It also leaves scars upon those who, for whatever reason, have been unable to rise with the mysterious leaven that has transported a majority in the West into the global middle class.

Class and snobbery

The long-term effects of the old industrial division of labor are not abolished simply because these have been declared off-limits by politicians and academics. They live on, in relationships and responses, and above all in people's sense of worth and self-esteem.

By 1851, more than half the English population lived in towns, and the country became the world's first urban nation. This was accompanied by the idealization of a rural past, which meant, for those with pretensions to the middle class, fleeing the conurbations for the refinement of a rural retreat. The children of the new rich were educated to lose all traces of their industrial origin, while their parents withdrew from the places where they had made their money, to live in imitation of the landed families.

Regional distinctions, in Britain, became class distinctions. It has taken five or six generations for these to fade. A few regions were less charged with industrial (and therefore, working-class) linguistic indicators, but in all the manufacturing areas, people were instantly classified as soon as they opened their mouths. This represented an enforced belonging, a sometimes reluctant identification with class. People 'betrayed' who they were, in spite of themselves.

An inability to speak 'properly' distinguished the British from the bilingual speakers of Italy or France, whose regional roots had far less to do with their class, and who moved from the dialect of Friuli or Provence into Italian or French according to context. This was impossible in Britain; and the social embarrassment, the crude classifying of people, the debilitating assumptions built into interpreting the speech of others continued to exercise its destructive influence on the lives of many people still living. Even now it marks out, to some degree, the 'underclass'; although the majority of people now speak what we might call Ukayese, the language of global markets, now universally acknowledged to be an international language, although in reality the dominant dialect of globalization.

The anguish 'an accent' created in people's interactions with their 'betters' is impossible to overstate; adults reduced to stammering incoherence in front of authority figures, unable to explain themselves to teachers, magistrates, employers, doctors; constantly diminished, their ideas dismissed, held to be of no account because they could not cope with the linguistic codes of their 'betters'; or erupting in violent action or abuse because no one was going to listen to them anyway. This still has the power to poison relationships and stifle interaction between people from different social backgrounds.

Perhaps the most pervasive embodiment of this inequality was to be found in the concept of 'snobbery'; an aspect of relationships between groups of people which has far from disappeared. Fittingly, the words 'snobbery' and 'snobbish' entered the language in the early industrial era. According to the Oxford Dictionary, a snob originally denoted 'a person belonging to the lower classes of society' (1852) and later 'one whose ideas and conduct are prompted by a vulgar admiration for wealth or social position'.

To such people was entrusted the task of the social policing of the poor and the working class; a duty they assumed with relish. It is no accident that in the contemporary world this task has devolved upon the expanding ranks of the middle classes all over the Third World. This development – the extension of modest privilege to a significant number – is the surest guarantor that they will support whatever needs to be done to preserve their position in the middle class and whatever is necessary to keep the poor in their place.

American dreams

The long-term consequences of the class-system in the US were explored by historians Richard Sennett and Jonathan Cobb[1] in 1972. From their study of Boston workers, they concluded that the ideology of individualism had eliminated any perception of society from the consciousness of the workers, but society had set up its conflicts within their personal lives; with the result that they took personal responsibility for the disappointment reserved for those who do not 'make it' according to the approved ideological theory. In other words, the structural injustices and inequalities had not gone away – they simply played themselves out on the territory of the personal lives of individuals – so that people would blame themselves for defeat and still acquiesce in the great social myths of equality.

Individualism makes people fight one another for dignity: 'In turning people against each other, the class system of authority and judgment-making goes itself into hiding; the system is left unchallenged as people enthralled by the enigmas of its power battle one another for respect.'

A prerequisite for this process is the dissolution of bonds of fraternity and recognition of a common predicament. Sennett and Cobb were looking at the decay of the old 'urban villages' of ethnic concentrations of Italians, Poles or Irish, as extended families gave way to limited nuclear groupings. These people then couldn't wait to escape the oppressive power of kinfolk and neighbors, and they moved to the suburbs in pursuit of freedoms that turned into loneliness. Networks of flesh and blood appeared as constraint rather than support. People began to work for their own children's emancipation from themselves. The analysis of this tragic process reveals much about the ways in which class has mutated in the US, and continues to haunt the lives of those who believe themselves free from its disciplines.

The workers interviewed by Sennett and Cobb expressed a defensive separation of their inner selves – the warm, loving aspect of their being – from the hard, cynical element they displayed in the work-place. Their creation of a life of dignity was increasingly placed in the future, and their children were to be the recipients of immense sacrifices.

Paradoxically, the desire was to make the children different from themselves, to bind them by gratitude while making them incapable of living the life they themselves had known. Betrayal was written into the treacherous scenario by which they conceived of rendering life more bearable. In this more subtle reading, class ambushes people in the inner sanctum of private life. Indeed the individual confronts the disabling power of class, and seeks to find personal remedies for humiliations inflicted by social and economic forces. This prescient work also foreshadows the same experience which came later to other Western societies.

In *Languages of Class*, Gareth Stedman Jones suggests that if its victims are to do anything about class distinctions, much depends on their ability to recognize and articulate the injustices they feel. Sennett and Cobb offer a convincing explanation of the disabling of what used to be called 'the working-class struggle'. It shows why class has ceased to be the object of an organized project, but has become the source of 'invisible' and unacknowledged violence, which continues to scar rich societies, in ways few can – or are willing to – recognize.

Onward and upward

Class – unlike caste – is distinguished by a certain amount of mobility. Upward mobility has been the experience of large numbers of (formerly) working class people since the 1950s; and although some people also come down, in Western society, upward mobility has been highly conspicuous in the reconstruction of a global working class.

This much publicized bettering of people seemed to have dissolved consciousness of class in the age of affluence in the 1950s and beyond. In 1959, Vance Packard's *The Status Seekers* sought to answer the question of what happens to class distinctions in a society where most people enjoy a prolonged period of material abundance. He forced open the celebrated 'disappearance of the class system in America' which was believed to have become 'one vast middle class'.

Packard wanted to show how the class system had been refined by the elaboration of status systems within it. The very proliferation of the goods and services that were to have caused class to wither away had become the focus of more subtle forms of re-defining and re-asserting class differences. He was writing at a time when 33 million Americans moved into a new neighborhood every year – an extraordinary rate of mobility. The need of people taking part in this epic gilded nomadism to establish their position, particularly in relation to those who share the same lifestyle, is carefully documented. They also need to create new precedences and hierarchies in the communities where they settle, to distinguish themselves from those they have left behind.

It seems that Packard was monitoring a shift in people's perception of themselves in relation to the productive process (where do the workers stand vis-à-vis the owners) in favor of a perception in relation to other people. As the division of labor became more complicated, more specialized and more internationalized, just who was who became more obscure. The symbols of superiority, of belonging and of status took on far greater importance in the lives of the people.

The ideology of competitive individualism flourished when the majority of people were mobile and detached from neighborhood: what people did became secondary to what they owned and possessed. People depended more and more for their income upon increasingly abstruse and abstract occupations. Who could have foreseen such functions in the global economy as a 'futures trader', as a monitor of 'invisibles' in imports and exports, of the importance of 'cultural products' in the global entertainment industry?

Packard's account of his status-seekers is both relevant and archaic. How much further it has gone by the beginning of the 21st century! The obsession with status has actually seeped down through the social structure, so that it is now a matter of great concern to young people, especially the deprived, that they should be seen to wear the 'correct' logos of transnational companies on their clothes. In the 1990s, stories emerged of teenagers even killing one another to gain possession of some coveted item of clothing. This represents a very serious redefinition of class, and equally, of class antagonism. For instance, if we look at the importance vested in ownership of clothing bearing the mark of Nike or Adidas, and we observe the conditions in which those goods are actually produced in Indonesia or Bangladesh, we shall quickly see that the status of the relatively low-income youth for whom such objects are significant depends directly on forms of servitude, even of semi-slavery, in the factories of South Asia. Examples of such dependency echo the position within Britain when even within living memory the makers of high-quality clothing, footwear and objects of consumption for the rich could not possibly afford the items which earned them a livelihood. My own family were workers in leather and shoes: they took pride in what they produced, even though the objects they made were beyond their means.

1 *The Hidden Injuries of Class*, Richard Sennett and Jonathan Cobb, Faber and Faber 1972.

8 Caste and class

An account of caste, using the model of India... Examining the effect of global integration upon this ancient form of social stratification... and then discussing the re-emergence of slavery and the institutionalizing of global social injustice.

CASTE SOCIETIES DIFFER from class societies in that positions are inherited and movement between castes does not occur. This was the way with the great majority of people in feudal Europe and has been even more marked in the hierarchies of caste in India.

India has in theory abolished Untouchability, under Article 17 of its Constitution. But socially this is a far greater task, simply because that system is an outcrop of a religious faith that cannot be wished away by decree. Indeed, there is much tension in India, precisely because a modern economy, incompatible with caste, has been pasted onto a more lasting décor of hierarchies, functions and duties of great antiquity. Although at odds with the India of Bollywood, the stock markets, information technology, high levels of consumption and all the attributes of the modern world, caste does not melt away. It is not entirely static, and certainly has been inflected by history: many Untouchables converted to Islam during the Mogul period. The British Raj also exploited casteism, and since Independence, successive governments have sought to lift up those disadvantaged by caste; while in an era of globalization, growing political organization by caste has been evident.

Ancient social conflict also mutates into economic struggle, and in a world of universal human rights, the defenders of caste-privilege are under attack. The policy of government 'reservations', that is, offering a certain proportion of government jobs and places in higher education to those traditionally disadvantaged by the caste system (notably Scheduled Castes and Scheduled

Tribes) created a powerful backlash by the higher castes, who invoke arguments about 'merit' to support their greater adaptability to the modern economic system, their superior access to the education and training that guarantee them a place in it.

The system in India was complicated by the legacy of the Raj. This left an élite whose knowledge of English – which has become the supreme vehicle of expression of economic dominance in the world – has enabled them to ally themselves with English-speaking élites in the global arena. The British, who built railways and roads, enforced cash-crop growing of indigo, jute and tea on subsistence farmers, undermined the function-based occupations of the caste-system, but also opened up new possibilities for education, as well as recruitment into the army and police.

However, upon older patterns of indigenous injustice modern inequalities were also superimposed: the coexistence of an industrializing economy with ancient methods of subsistence and self-reliance makes statistics doubly unreliable. The often-quoted 1.2 billion people living on less than a dollar a day is a misleading index of poverty, since self-reliance means sufficiency outside of the market economy. Statistics based upon market-measured poverty discredit traditional ways of measuring well-being, and they also assume that the future of people existing outside, or only partially within the global market, will be of total inclusion within it. This offers some clue to the impossibility of 'solving' problems of poverty following the prescriptions of the single 'integrated' economy now consolidating itself across the whole world.

How it began

The caste-system is believed to have evolved out of the conquest of Aryan or Indo-European invaders of the darker Dravidians, while at the same time absorbing some of their proto-caste hierarchies. In the middle of the first millennium BC, caste inequalities became more clearly demarcated and institutionalized, and were legitimized with the rise of Brahmanic Hinduism, and formalized in the laws of Manu, in which subjection of women and discrimination against the Sudras were explicit.

The four major caste formations in India ramify into enormous numbers of sub-divisions. The basic castes are called *varnas* or colors; sub-castes, or *jatis* are subdivisions of the *varnas*. The Brahmin, or priestly caste is at the apex, with the Kshatriya or warrior caste next, followed by the Vaishyas, or merchants and traders, and then the Sudras, who are laborers and servants.

Those outside the formal caste-groups, the Untouchables, are now known as Dalits, the oppressed. Traditionally, contact with such people was considered polluting, and elaborate purification rituals were necessary before social relationships with one's own caste could be re-established. It is significant that the lowest castes were, in one way or another, connected with the most basic functions of human existence – the removers of waste, those working with dead animals and leather, fishing communities, those dealing with sickness and death, conservers of the environment. The most indispensable people were considered to be 'polluters'. There is an epic paradox in this: given the ravages imposed by industrialism on the planet, it is to such people we must now look for inspiration in recycling and conserving resources. Their rejection by the caste-system is one of the peculiar bequests of India to the modern world, to an omnivorous industrialism that cannot demolish the resources of the earth quickly enough.

The Indian system of caste is perhaps the most tenacious of all hierarchies. The sanction they take from religion embeds them profoundly in a society to which they give meaning. The *Bhagavad Gita* states that the work of a Brahmin is peace, austerity and purity; loving-forgiveness and righteousness; vision, wisdom and faith. The work of a Kshatriya is a heroic mind, inner fire, constancy, resourcefulness, courage in battle, generosity and noble leadership. The work of a Vaishya is trade, agriculture and the rearing of cattle. The work of the Sudra is service. Beneath them are the Untouchables. It is significant that the higher castes are distinguished by their qualities, or virtues, the lower by their function. In this they resemble the division of industrial society into upper, lower and *working* classes.

The first three *varnas* are twice-born. This means simply coming to religious maturity, able to study the *Vedas* (holy texts), perform Vedic rites and study Sanskrit. It occurs for boys at the age of 8 for Brahmins, 11 for Kshatriyas and 12 for Vaishyas. The equivalent for girls comes with marriage.

For the twice-born, there are four stages of life. First, *brahmacharya*, or student, who lives with a teacher, is obedient, chaste and non-violent. The second is the *gharastya*, or householder, whose duty is to perform the principal *dharma* (religious observance), while a woman carries out the duties of wife and mother. The third stage is the *vanaprastya*, or forest-dweller, when, the duties of family fulfilled, possessions are surrendered, and religious rituals reduced to a minimum. The final stage is that of *sanyasin*, or wandering ascetic, although this applies only to men (women return home). The *sanyasin* has renounced the world completely, and is beyond religion and caste.

The Sudras, once-born, are not supposed to study Sanskrit or the *Vedas*. Their function is to serve the twice-born. The Untouchables or outcastes, are ritually polluting to caste Hindus. They comprise around 17 per cent of the Hindus. Gandhi called them Harijans, literally, children of God, but more recently, they have taken on the name of Dalits.[1]

In theory, a system of caste status-ascription standing in the way of the modern world, ought to disintegrate under the necessities of globalization. It hasn't been so simple: ancient cultures do not necessarily immediately relinquish their customs because of an economic necessity decreed from elsewhere. There has been a greater assertiveness and organization by Dalits for political inclusion, access to education and government employment. But more general social advancement is much slower. Outrages against such people are commonplace, and it is not unusual now for revenge attacks on higher castes by Dalits, sometimes creating localized civil strife, especially in the villages of Bihar, Madhya Pradesh and the remoter parts of Uttar Pradesh. In response to this, the rise of the Hindu Right and its fundamentalist underpinning, has sought to turn back the rise of the Dalits. However since this has to operate in a democratic system, where the majority are not in the upper castes and where a Muslim minority of about 12 per cent of the population must be accommodated, this is no easy task. In this context, fundamentalisms, both Islamic and Hindu, nourish each other. The question of how far both are a response to the spread of Western economic fundamentalism remains a question far from resolved.

The impact of caste on the lives of the people is multi-dimensional. It controls their occupation in a static division of labor. It prohibits marriage outside of the caste: to marry out is to expel both parties from their respective castes. Since the caste-system is an aspect of religion, an outcrop of the informing belief that makes Hinduism cohere, it cannot be dismantled by administrative, bureaucratic or even humanitarian decree. The closed worlds of caste retain a powerful hold over the people.

The word Dalit applies to those officially designated by the Indian Government as 'Scheduled Castes and Tribes', as well as to neo-Buddhists (many of whom converted under the influence of Dalit leader Dr Ambedkar, who despaired of reform in Independent India), the landless and poor peasants, all those exploited politically, economically and in the name of religion. Efforts to create political parties to represent the Untouchables culminated in the formation by politican Kanshi Ram of the Bahujan Samaj Party, which briefly took control of the government of Uttar Pradesh in 1995, supported for a time by the BJP (the Hindu communalist party now in government in India).

Almost 90 per cent of Dalits live in the rural areas, usually segregated from the rest of the village. More than half are landless agricultural laborers and in 1971 the literacy rate was 14.7 per cent compared to 29.5 per cent of the rest of the population. Even within Untouchability, hierarchies have developed, whereby some groups regard themselves as superior to others: the *chambhar* regard the *mahar* as inferior, and these regard the *mang* as even lower. Each year, there are at least 10,000 acts of violence against Untouchables. Every hour two Dalits are assaulted; every day three Dalit women are raped; every day two Dalits are murdered and two Dalit houses are burned down.

Dalits were ritually polluting: it was a sin for caste Hindus to look at them, to talk to them, even to have their shadow fall on them. They were compelled to live outside the village, forbidden to wear gold, silver or jewels. They had to wear the clothes of the dead. They could not share food with caste Hindus or even draw water from the same well. They were not allowed to enter temples. They were excluded from education. Many of their traditional tasks are becoming obsolete, so many have become jobless. They have remained so far outside of mainstream communication systems that many do not even know that there is legislation outlawing Untouchability. They remain among the poorest people in India; starvation deaths and prostitution affect Untouchables more than any other group.

Caste-relations are being re-shaped by urbanization, migration, education and technological change. They were never quite as rigid as has been believed: like all human institutions, capable of both fixity and flexibility. But the image of closed worlds is a powerful one. In India, the existence side by side of a modern industrial and commercial sector with an older agrarian caste-society creates a kind of apartheid. While migration to towns and cities is a constant and usually one-way process, more than three-quarters of India's population remain rural. And even the life of the cities is dominated by divisions which, in some measure, reproduce the separations of an older way of life.

Tradition versus hi-tech

I was in Bangalore in March 2001, hi-tech capital of India, focus of both hope and hype about the future of the country. There are enclaves of self-contained luxury. Companies have their own generators in place of an erratic public electricity supply. They have swimming pools, gymnasia, tennis courts and all kinds of facilities for their personnel. There are five-star hotels for the benefit of visitors from the US, Australia and Europe. There are clubs and pubs, discos and department stores which give an impression that Bangalore is indeed a flagship of the future; that its energy and dynamism will ripple out and transform, if not the whole country, then at least the state of Karnataka of which it is the capital.

It isn't like that. In the *Deccan Herald* of March 9th 2001, there was a report that four members of a family committed suicide by taking poison at Belar Taluk. They were upset over the daughter eloping with her lover. The family members had disapproved of the marriage, which drove the lovers to run away. The deceased were a man and wife, aged 50, and their sons, 27 and 23. The daughter was in love with their neighbor's son. When this boy approached the girl's father and sought his approval for the marriage, the latter turned him down.

This is also Karnataka, site of hope and deliverance for the people of India. Outside the enclosures of modernity, life continues an age-old pattern. It is not easy for those enclosed within a world of futuristic technology to appreciate the state of mind that drives, not only parents, but two vigorous and healthy sons to kill themselves out of a shame that surely belongs to the past.

It is hard to imagine such an apparently archaic sensibility, that makes the family prefer suicide to survival when a girl elopes with a lover of choice. It is clear traditional societies do not give up so easily. They are, however, inflected by the influence of the modern world, and in doing so may become even more hardened and extreme. This has significant implications when we discuss culture and its role in human lives. Reductive arguments about poverty, as interpreted through the statistics of financial institutions and international agencies, lose their power in the presence of such awesome and ancient values.

Slavery

India, too, is one of the principal places in the world where bonded labor persists; a form of slavery, often inherited by children for debts contracted with moneylenders at extortionate interest by their parents or grandparents. Indeed, not only does traditional slavery continue in the modern world, but new forms of enslavement are occurring; with the result that there are at present more slaves in the world than there were at the time of its formal abolition.

From the late 15th century, millions of Africans were transported to the Americas to work on plantations producing sugar, tobacco, cotton and cocoa for European markets. Much of the wealth of Europe was built on slavery, as the elegant cities of Liverpool and Bristol testified. The slave trade was formally abolished in Britain in 1807. The Anti-Slavery Society was founded in 1823, and the Slavery Abolition

Act was passed in 1833. The American Anti-Slavery Society was founded in 1833 and abolition decreed from 1863, with the resistance in the South that led to the Civil War. Of course, in reality slavery persisted much longer. Like many other ancient abuses, it has taken on new forms in the modern world.

According to the United Nations High Commissioner for Human Rights, The word 'slavery' today covers a variety of human rights violations. In addition to traditional slavery and the slave trade, these abuses include the sale of children, child prostitution, exploitation of child labor, sexual mutilation of female children, use of children in armed conflicts, debt bondage, the traffic in persons and the sale of human organs, prostitution. Slavery-like practices may be clandestine. There is enough evidence, however, to show that these are widespread and on a vast scale. Just one figure tells a grim story: 100 million children are exploited for their labor, according to a recent estimate by the International Labour Organization.

Ship of slaves

11 June 2001. Gabon police arrested the man responsible for chartering the *Etireno*, which was carrying dozens of children into slavery. Stanislas Abatan, from Benin, and five men from Togo and Benin who were his accomplices, were arrested at the end of May. The Nigerian-registered boat captured international attention after it was reported to be carrying children into slavery. Twenty-three children, aged between three and fourteen, were rescued in Benin on 17 April as they were being trafficked to Gabon for work. They were at sea for more than two weeks because the boat was forced to return to Benin after Cameroon and Gabon refused it permission to dock. According to French aid organization *Terre des Hommes*, which has been interviewing and caring for the young children, the eight boys and 15 girls came from Benin, Mali and Togo. In interview, five children said that there were financial transactions before their departure and eight confirmed they were traveling with an unfamiliar adult. Eighteen of the 23 children said they were being taken to Gabon to work. ■

Anti-Slavery International.

Early in 2000, I sat in a Dhaka hotel lobby with a man who was recruiting labor in Bangladesh for a factory in the United Arab Emirates (UAE). He said in Bangladesh work was interrupted by political strikes and inadequate infrastructure. By locating his factory in UAE, he would have a captive workforce, which could not speak the language, which would work virtually unlimited hours under threat of instant dismissal and have no distractions from their labor. He said 'What I am doing is a form of slavery. It should not happen. But nothing prevents me from doing it.'

Bonded labor, particularly in South Asia, is still widespread, despite formal prohibition. Many bonded laborers in rural India enter into unofficial contracts for the sake of loans for marriage, dowry or medicines. These are often of limited duration, and employers force them to say they are free labor. With no evidence of compulsion, collusion occurs between the exploiters and exploited

In July 2000, the Government of Nepal abolished the *kamaiya* system of bonded labor, which affected about 100,000 of the ethnic Tharus. Many landlords expelled the laborers from their land, even though they were entitled to keep their houses and a portion of the land they farmed. The displaced people are living in emergency camps, where they have no access to clean water and food. No formal legislation has yet been passed outlawing debt bondage, and no provisions have been made to ensure the rights of those released. Few have been granted even the minimum land (0.4 hectares) required for household survival. Some 7,000 *kamaiya* families have occupied government or forest land in order to grow their own crops. Many of their huts have been burned and leaders of the evicted communities arrested.

The growth of a global middle class

This is what the bland phrase 'growing inequality' actually means. While the poorest are increasingly

Soldiering on

While it is easy to find a table of the 20 richest people in the world (see Chapter 1), it would be impossible to do the same with the 20 poorest. But certainly, among the most degraded and enslaved, we might include child soldiers.

'An estimated 14,000 children in northern Uganda have been abducted and turned into soldier-slaves by the rebel Lord's Resistance Army (LRA). More than 90 per cent of the LRA's troops are children – terrorized through violence, sexual abuse and threats, then forced to kill. Many die at the hands of the LRA or in skirmishes with government forces. Those who escape are severely traumatized. They can face rejection by their communities and may be charged with treason by the Government.

'These slave-soldiers are not restricted to Uganda. The United Nations estimates nearly 300,000 children between 10 and 17 have been forced into toting guns at the behest of rebel groups or governments in 30 countries'. ■

New Internationalist, No. 337 August 2001.

deprived of both liberty and livelihood, at the same time a new rich class has grown and developed with global economic integration. Existing élites have links with the wider world. They own property abroad, have bank accounts in Western countries. Their children go to the US, Australia or Europe for higher education. The family spends part of the year abroad. Their lives are articulated to their own country in the most limited ways, unless they are actually in government. Their peers are the privileged of other countries and their life-style scarcely different from that of their Western counterparts. This is a relatively small group – maybe 2,000 interconnected families who have key positions in business, politics, academic life, or the media.

I traveled from Dhaka to London in the spring of 2000 and because I had a broken ankle I went Business Class. I was astonished at the number of people who greeted each other. Some were going to Karachi, others to London, yet others on to New York and Los Angeles. The cabin quickly came to resemble a sort of cocktail party, with people circulating in order to exchange anecdotes, news and gossip with their acquaintances. I felt I had intruded on a private occasion, in which everyone else was part of a narrow network of privilege.

Below this small circle of international travelers, there is also a growing middle class, for whom these notables serve as model and inspiration. They do not have the means to compete, but they mimic their life-style in a more modest way. Their children go to expensive schools. In Bangladesh, for example, they have maids, drivers and cooks; they shop in Bangkok or Hong Kong, go to Calcutta or Mumbai for medical treatment and their children work in Singapore or the US. Some will have amassed a certain capital in the Gulf, which they have invested in business, construction, a garments factory, buying-house or import business, dealing in fabrics from Taiwan or China, or goods of almost any kind from India.

Characteristically, in these countries, the richest 20 per cent of the population will gain around two-thirds of the annual income. The poorest 20 per cent will earn between 4 and 10 per cent. These proportions are similar to the income distribution in Germany or the US, where, according to the *World Bank Development Report 2000*, the poorest 20 per cent get 11.5 per cent and 7 per cent respectively. [These proportions do not indicate ownership of assets and wealth, which, of course, significantly advantages the rich even further.] In India, the poorest 20 per cent receive 11.6 per cent of annual income – in theory, making it less unjust than the US.

But since the income differential is so great, poverty in India has a quite different meaning from poverty in America. This demonstrates another deficiency in dependency upon statistics, and the importance of recovering a sense of the *relationships* between rich and poor, if the poor are to make meaningful gains. This cannot be done without a strong feeling of moral revulsion against injustice and this is absent from the modern world, blunted as it has been by the iconography of universal wealth and prosperity which dominates the media in every country.

There is no lack of publicity dissecting the maldistribution of rewards in the world. Robert Reich, former Secretary of Labor in the US Government, said on the eve of the Millennium that in 1999 the richest 2.7 million Americans (the top one per cent) would have as many after-tax dollars to spend as the bottom 100 million put together. Meanwhile, the poorest one-fifth of households would have an average income of $8,800, down from $10,000 in 1977 (in current dollars). That's about £6,600 down to £5,800 in sterling.

The numbers game

The aid agency Oxfam opened its briefing on the options for the new Millennium with a reassertion that 1.2 billion people live on less than a dollar a day. This measurement of poverty is not only a fatalistic acceptance that poverty equals a purely monetary sum, but it also ensures that poverty will never be eradicated. For in a world of growing inequality, as long as the rich go on getting richer, poverty will simply become more and more relative: in 50 years' time, Oxfam will doubtless be publishing bulletins

---

Life expectancy

While life expectancy has increased from 48 in 1855, it is now 68, and by 2025 is expected to be 75. Twenty-one million children died before the age of five in 1955. Forty years later the figure had gone down to 11 million, and by 2025 it will be reduced to 5 million. The estimated 600,000 women who die from complications in pregnancy or in child-birth each year has remained static. AIDS is now the major cause of death in sub-Saharan Africa. Life expectancy in Botswana rose from under 43 years in 1955 to 61 years in 1990, but with between 25-30 per cent of the adult population infected with HIV, life expectancy is expected to drop to levels last seen in the 1960s. By 2010, Zimbabwe's infant mortality is expected to rise by 138 per cent because of AIDS; and under-five mortality by 109 per cent. ■

Oxfam UK

containing the shocking statistic that 2 billion or 4 billion people in the world are living on less than $10 (£6) a day; a statistic which will be as outrageous to the enlightened of the future as it is to the numbed of the present.

As long as inequality grows, perceptions of what poverty is will always come limping behind wealth. It will be impossible to determine what constitutes a decent security, a safe sufficiency. What might constitute *enough* for human beings has been written out of the global scenario; and so has what might be possible outside and beyond market economics.

There is no barrier to the growth and expansion of the global economy, to which all humanity must now look for hope; although the destructive weight of this on the planet is becoming more and more clear. The generation of wealth is more important than the regeneration of the planet, as George W Bush made clear when he rejected the Kyoto protocol in 2001. The creation of money has a higher priority than the procreation of humanity. The growth of the economy takes precedence over the malignant growth of an incurable poverty; incurable because indefinable, the outcrop of a system that has set free infinite desire in a finite world.

The Oxfam briefing remarks that the countries which have performed strongest on poverty reduction – China, Malaysia and Thailand – have experienced marked increases in inequality; a trend which is even more marked on the global scale. Citing the UN Development Program's 1999 *Human Development Report*, it repeats that one-fifth of the people in the world have 86 per cent per cent of world GDP; 82 per cent of world export markets; and 68 per cent of foreign direct investment. The poorest fifth had one per cent in each case. The world's richest 200 people more than doubled their wealth to one trillion dollars between 1994 and 1998. The assets of the top three billionaires came to more than the combined GDP of all least developed countries and their 600 million people. By 1998, the top ten companies in pesticides controlled 85 per cent of a $31 billion global market; and the top 10 in telecommunications, 86 per cent of a $262 billion market.

At the end of the 1990s, over 125 million children of primary school age were denied education by being out of school. About 150 million more will drop out before becoming literate. Girls make up two-thirds of those out of school, and account for most of those

---

'We are everywhere!'

By 2001, almost half the world's population had become urban. This means that 40 per cent or more of the people are still peasants, small farmers, subsistence growers, indigenous peoples. No significant change in the world can occur without their participation. In January 1994, in the state of Chiapas in Southern Mexico, descendants of the former great Mayan civilization – now mostly reduced to poverty and landlessness – came out of the Lacandon jungle and seized the towns of San Cristobal de Las Casas and Ocosingo. The Zapatista National Liberation Army was born (named after Emilio Zapata, who fought for indigenous land rights in the early 20th century). The Mexican oil boom of the 1970s drew many migrants away from the area, and traditional farming practices were abandoned. Following the debt crisis of 1982, many returned, bringing with them new methods of agriculture, relying on fertilizer and pesticides. This degraded the fragile land rapidly and led to environmental disaster.

Out of this impoverishment the Zapatista movement was born; defying government and setting up its own autonomous rule in the areas controlled by the people, under the leadership of the highly articulate sub-comandante Marcos. There were hundreds of deaths in the mid and late 1990s, as they resisted attempts by the army to destroy their movement.

In March 2001, there was a march on the capital, Mexico City, a March of Indigenous Dignity, to press for the passage of a law on indigenous rights and culture. Scores of thousands of people in the capital greeted the Zapatistas as heroes. Government hardliners called them 'terrorists', and the law recognizing the rights and culture of indigenous peoples was dramatically scaled down, withdrawing the promises of autonomy and self-determination. The low-intensity war resumed. But the Zapatistas have inspired the world as an example of popular resistance to centuries of discrimination which has been exacerbated by the asperities of globalization. ■

dropping out.

In the division of labor in the world, it is still women who bear the greatest burden. They make up 51 per cent of the agricultural labor force, and characteristically work 12 hours a day, compared with the 8 or 10 hours worked by men. In some regions women spend up to 5 hours a day collecting fuelwood and water, and 4 hours preparing food. In Africa, 90 per cent of the work of collecting water and wood for the household and for food is done by women. In the least developed countries 23 per cent of households are headed by women.

The Oxfam report concludes: 'There must be a sea-change in aid, debt relief and trade policies if the international development target of halving poverty is to be achieved. The tragedy is that the future need not be so bleak. We have the wealth, knowledge and resources to make the next millennium a prosperous one for all. What is lacking is the vision and commitment to provide an equitable health service, clean water, a basic education system and an equitable share of the world's resource to the poor.'

1 Caste: *Untouchable! Voices of the Dalit Liberation Movement*, Barbara Joshi, Zed Books 1986; *Politics of the Depressed Classes*, Trilok Nath, Deputy Publications Delhi 1982; *Dalits and the Democratic Revolution*, Gail Omvedt, Sage New Delhi 1994.

9 Conclusion

How class as a basis for social liberation is being overtaken by globalization, from which a more profound human emancipation is in the process of being formulated.

IN ALMOST ALL reports on poverty with their diagnoses and analyses, there is a use of the first person plural. What *we* know, what *we* can do, what *we* must do, if disaster is to be avoided (apart from the disaster that has wiped out an incalculable number of lives since *we* began collecting such information). This treacherous pronoun suggests what has been articulated, namely the existence of 'an international community', an entity which the Oxfam report also invokes. This inclusive fiction is seen as a kind of appeal of last resort, implying a universal commitment to humanity, justice and freedom.

Alas, it doesn't exist. What the international community is committed to is an ideology, and one moreover that has defeated the principal agent of transforming change. The beneficiaries, controllers and administrators of the global economy are dedicated to the propagation of the ideology of growth and expansion in perpetuity; and this is the sine qua non of a globalization which is promoted as though it were a force of nature, suggesting that there is neither escape from nor an alternative to the structure which has been built upon its basic premises. For the world to be in thrall to a single ideology is doubtless a powerful solvent of conflict, if only you can get the whole world voluntarily to assent to it. But this is the ideology of the powerful. And their fortunes have been spectacularly advanced in the past decade, following the death of the only threat to that ideology – embodied in the Soviet Union.

Now the gain to the world by the existence of this monstrosity was slender in the extreme. In fact it was not from the ideology of communism that any notable benefit accrued to humanity in general; but the loss of that alternative has been an impoverishment indeed – not only for the extinction of diversity in economic matters, but also because nothing is left to inhibit the system left in place after the disappearance of the Soviet system. The extinction of communism removed the last constraint on the exuberant self-promotion and development of global capitalism. Today this goes under the alias of globalization, to which all alternatives have been noisily annulled by the only voices now heard in the world – the voices of wealth and privilege. It is on their terms, according to their say-so, in accordance with their wishes that all the pious utterances on poverty abatement, justice and democracy are now licensed.

The world is caught in a terrible trap, of which the deceptive monosyllable of the first person plural is both symbol and expression. A whole structure of coercion and violence is built into its fateful simplicity. For the inclusive plural *we* means no such thing; it is the voice of power, and it dictates the terms that any improvements in the world must not disturb the serene enjoyment of the advantages which we – and our dependents and supporters – pursue. If what you desire is incompatible with that necessity, it will be suppressed.

It is no good arguing that there is enough food in the world for no one to go hungry. Useless to say that nothing could be simpler than to divert a fraction of the money spent on armaments to the relief of poverty. Pointless to get passionate about the ease with which all the available drugs could be made available to all the HIV-affected in the world without material damage to the profits of drug companies. If these things cannot be accomplished within the existing mechanisms, they will not be accomplished at all.

We can now begin to see exactly how the loss of class consciousness has affected the world. Losing consciousness is a troubling experience at the best of times; particularly if, when you come round, you find you are in an unfamiliar place, where the landscape is unknown, everything is strangely altered. We are in the land of the great mythic sleepers of folklore and literature – Rip van Winkle, Sleeping Beauty, the drinking of the waters of Lethe, the arms of Morpheus – epics of amnesia, the effects of opiates and the 'end of history'. The changes that have occurred in the world are all external, technological, the tearing down and reconstruction of the human-made environment: they have not changed the enduring and fateful relationship between rich and poor. Only the reconstruction of class on the global scale is no longer recognized as identical with its earlier, national versions. It has taken on the abstract sheen of inequality.

The separation, dispersal and scattering of the global working class, and the consequent loss of consciousness, does not change their position in relation to the global rich and middle classes. It is true that the world may be spared the spectacle of global class warfare. But what it will not be proof against is the kind of distortions that are already clearly visible, a kind of in-turned guerrilla warfare. These conflicting interests will continue to express themselves, in social disorder and breakdown, ethnic and religious strife, increasing crime, both organized and opportunistic, violent struggles over resources, the establishment of private armies to defend the privacy of wealth, and the growth of banditry by the rich in pursuit of privilege and by the poor in pursuit of survival. The consciousness of any pattern behind such apparently random and mindless violence may have been lost; but its effects in the world are all too plain.

Action against inequality

This brings us back to the question posed at the beginning of the book: why is there so little effective action against inequalities which are well documented and well known?

If the interests of rich and poor are incompatible, it is to do no favors to the poor to preach the virtues of patience and forbearance. However, given the apparatus of repression at the disposal of the powerful, it would also be foolish to preach revolution, uprising or any other form of violence. This stalemate reflects a deeper dilemma in the contemporary world – the conflicting ideas that everything cannot go on like this (resource-abuse, degradation of the elements that sustain life, the extinction of flowers, trees, animals and human cultures alike), and that it cannot not go on like this (since it provides the great majority of humankind with a livelihood, the means of survival). Nothing is better calculated to lead to a sense of paralysis and impotence.

In this context, it is not to the emancipation of this or that class we should look for salvation. Neither the overthrow of the global order by the working class, nor the perpetuation of it by the possessing classes offers an adequate prospect for the future of the world and its peoples. Yet the potential for a more fully human liberation exists in some of the popular movements of hope in the world. The poor who survive on so little, with their frugality, recycling, eking out a living on next to nothing, offer a model of resource-conservation and modest demands, while the vast productive power of the global economy provides more than enough for an easy sustenance of all people on earth.

If these cannot come together in a common endeavor for the deliverance not only of a working class or the poor – and equally of those weighed down by the burdensome iconography of a depowering wealth, a fearful defense of a privilege which depends upon human sacrifice for its maintenance – then what may be expected is a future of increasing violence, resource-wars, crime, the establishment of private armies to defend the privacy of unjustly distributed wealth, the growth of global banditry in the interests of private remedies to growing social injustice. The alternative is a secure sufficiency for all, a modest prosperity and the recovery of *enough* to satisfy the needs of all humanity.

It is unlikely that recognition of a common destiny will lead to a reconciliation of rich and poor; particularly when the dynamic which propels the global system involves an ever-growing divide between them. But without it, the conflict of classes which has scarred the industrial era will be as nothing to the levels of degradation and cruelty that lie in wait for the world: these will render the asperities of both feudalism and class society benign interludes by comparison with the strife to come.

Of course, history is never concluded in this world. To believe otherwise is the error into which both the unimaginative and pedestrian inheritors of Marx and the triumphal victors of global capital have, at different times, fallen. Struggle has not been canceled by the apparent impregnable strength of the globalizing imperative; not even that between newly constituted possessing and wanting classes of the world, whose antagonism refuses to lie down in the shallow graves of a frightened and decaying imperialism.

That the project of the Left has been canceled should not dismay those working for a more equitable world. The new movements for social justice comprehend a far wider range of people. They include the Zapatistas of Chiapas in Mexico; the farmers resisting transnational seed companies in India; those agitating against genetically modified crops in Europe; the movements of workers and their Western allies in the factories of big brand-names and logos in Asia, Central and South America; the resistance to the McDonaldization and Disneyfication of the cultures of the globe; the organization of

Conclusion

indigenous peoples all over the world; the transnational cooperation of the urban poor; the return to organic farming in the rich world; the resistance against a florid consumerism; the defense of small-scale cultures; and the revaluing of local production and administration against centralization.

Above all, we are seeing the rescue of internationalism from globalization by those bearing witness against the secretive cabals of the rich in their fortified enclaves in Seattle, Prague, Nice, Genoa or wherever they hold their macabre conventions. If the dictatorship of the proletariat is dead, this is only, perhaps, to make way for a wider emancipation of humanity.

CONTACTS

It is perhaps not surprising that the politics of class should have deserted mainstream parties and class-based socialist groupings, and should find itself now embodied in non-government organizations, pressure groups and international movements for social justice. Here are a few of which I have had some experience.

Drop The Debt. This successor to Jubilee 2000 is calling for deeper cancellation of Third World debt, including 100 per cent from the International Monetary Fund and the World Bank for the poorest countries of Africa, Latin America and Asia. It is supported by CAFOD, Christian Aid, the Mothers' Union, Oxfam, Tearfund, UNISON and the World Development Movement.
Email: www.dropthedebt.org

War on Want. This important agency campaigning against poverty, for social justice and equitable development is fifty years old. It supports workers, particularly women workers, in some of the most exploited areas of the world.
Fenner Brockway House, 37–39 Great Guildford Street, London SE1 OES, UK.
Email: mailroom@waronwant.org

Consumers' Association of Penang. One of the foremost global campaigners against global social injustice and Western dominance through its ideology of consumerism and individualism. Originator of the alternative news agency, Third World Network, Third World Resurgence, and campaigns against the power of the transnationals. 228 Macalister Road, Penang 10400, Malaysia.

World Development Movement. Founded in 1970 to tackle the root causes of poverty, it has branches all over the United Kingdom.
25 Beehive Place, London SW9 7QR, UK. Email: wdm@wdm.org.uk

Alliance for Democracy. Opposition to the corporate dominance of the US.
681 Main Street, Waltham, MA 02451 US.
Email: peoplesall@aol.com

Human Rights Watch. Protects human rights around the world, supporting victims and activists to bring offenders to justice. Works to prevent discrimination, uphold political freedom and to protect people from inhumane conduct in wartime. Seeks to hold human rights abusers to account.
350 Fifth Avenue, New York NY 10118-3291, US.
Email: hrwnyc@hrw.org.

Food First/Institute for Food and Development Policy. 398 60th Street, Oakland, California CA 94618, US.
Email: foodfirst@foodfirst.org

One World International. Dedicated to the promotion of human rights and sustainable development.
Floor 17, 89 Albert Embankment, London SE1 7TP, UK.
Email: justice@oneworld.net

Anti-Slavery International. The Stableyard, Broomgrove Road, London SW9 9TL, UK.

Contacts / Bibliography

International Society for Ecology and Culture. Movement for local regeneration, the protection of local cultures, ecologies and communities, which grew out of the work of Helena Norberg-Hodge in Ladakh in North India.
Apple Barn, Week, Totnes, Devon TQ9 6JP, UK.
www.ecovillages.org/india/ladakh

Research Foundation for Science, Technology and Ecology. Founded by environmentalist and campaigner Vandana Shiva. Address; A-60 Hauz Khas, New Delhi 100016, India.
www.indiaserver.com/betas/shiva

National Alliance of People's Movements. c/o Shram Sadhana D.V. Pradhan Road, Hindu Colony, Dadar East, Mumbai 400 014, India. Tel: +91 22 414 2918/ 414 4336.

National Campaign on Dalit Human Rights. A campaign to ensure Dalit issues are addressed by the UN World Conference Against Racism, Racial Discrimination, Xenophobia and Racial Intolerance. 2nd Floor, Duma Building, 1-8-142B 3rd Cross, Prendergast Road, Secunderabad 560 003 India.
Email: info@dalits.org

Bibliography

Capital, Karl Marx (Lawrence and Wishart, 1977).

Change in British Society, A Halsey (Oxford University Press, 1986).

Class and Class Conflict in Industrial Society, T Dahrendorf (Routledge and Kegan Paul, 1959).

The Coming of Post-Industrial Society, D Bell (Basic Books, 1973).

Divisions of Labour, R Pahl (Basil Blackwell, 1984).

Hidden from History, Sheila Rowbotham (Pluto Press, 1973).

Relative Deprivation and Social Justice, W Runciman (Routledge and Kegan Paul, 1966).

The Road to Wigan Pier, George Orwell (Gollancz, 1934).

A Seventh Man, John Berger (Penguin, 1975).

White Collar, CW Mills (Oxford University Press, 1951).

Wigan Pier Revisited, Beatrice Campbell (Virago, 1984).

Working Class Community, B Jackson (Routledge and Kegan Paul, 1968).

Index

Index